FORGET the Anorak

WHAT TRAINSPOTTING
WAS REALLY LIKE

MICHAEL G. HARVEY

The History Press

First published in 2004 by Sutton Publishing

This edition first published in 2009
Reprinted 2010, 2011, 2017

The History Press
The Mill, Brimscombe Port
Stroud, Gloucestershire, GL5 2QG
www.thehistorypress.co.uk

British Library Cataloguing in Publication Data.
A catalogue record for this book is available from the British Library.

ISBN 978 0 7524 5326 2

Typesetting and origination by The History Press
Printed in India.

Contents

Acknowledgements

Ian Allan Publishing
Frank Allen
Denis Callender
Fionna Coles
Margaret Condon
David Copus (the late)
Jeni & Dave Darkins
The Dockyard Historical Trust
Tony Genower
Leslie Hyde (the late)
D.K. Jones Collection
John Kinchen
George Lee
Ray Masterton

Brian Mould
David Neil
Norman E. Preedy
David Rendell
Gordon K. Roberts
Trevor Robson
Eddie Rooke
Stephen Sainsbury
Sam Savage
Graham Scott
Allan Sommerfield Collection
John Spence
Ron White, Colour-Rail
Doug Willis

Unless otherwise indicated, all photographs and line drawings are by the author.

Preface

The 1950s and 1960s were the heyday of trainspotting. It did exist before the Second World War, but it was the advent of the Ian Allan ABC Locospotters books from the late 1940s that really gave the hobby its impetus, providing an easy way of recording engine numbers in inexpensive pocket-sized books which were produced in large numbers.

The railways of Britain were particularly attractive to spotters in this period, and when the transition from steam to diesel and electric came about in the early and mid-1960s it provided immense variety and interest. For many trainspotters, however, the end of BR steam in 1968 was followed by a somewhat rapid decline of interest in the hobby and its less than total replacement by a more generalised railway enthusiasm.

By the mid-1950s trainspotting had become an organised hobby for those who wished to participate along those lines, and railway clubs provided cheap trips to virtually every corner of our railway system, which could result in anything up to eight days away from home.

For trainspotters to pursue their hobby vigorously they had to earn money for trips. Some kind of work was essential; for some this included an apprenticeship; for others it required odd jobs at weekends and evenings to bring in extra pocket money.

Glossary

For the benefit of non-railway enthusiasts, the following list explains some of the terms used in this book:

bunking	illegal entry to railway installations
cabbed	actually climbing up into a cab of a locomotive
cop	noting a certain locomotive for the first time
DMU	Diesel Multiple Unit
GWR	Great Western Railway
LMSR	London Midland & Scottish Railway
LNER	London & North Eastern Railway
LSWR	London & South Western Railway
Mogul	a steam locomotive with a 2–6–0 wheel arrangement
on shed	refers to the number of locomotives actually noted at one particular depot
Pacific	a steam locomotive with a 4–6–2 wheel arrangement
permit	an official letter authorising a visit to a locomotive depot or works
Pompey	Portsmouth Football Club
Prairie	a steam locomotive with a 2–6–2 wheel arrangement
shed	another term for a locomotive depot
SR	Southern Railway pre-nationalisation; Southern Region post-nationalisation
WD	a War Department steam locomotive
WR	Western Region

Introduction

The hobby of trainspotting in the 1950s and 1960s, in the days when steam trains ruled the British Railways system, was without a doubt a most fascinating, rewarding and healthy pastime. It certainly kept us teenagers off the streets of Portsmouth and out of any mischief, and it gave us an interesting hobby – one that we could easily and happily share with our school companions. As it transpired, many of my closest friends who shared this interest actually gained employment with British Railways when they left school and in subsequent years they worked their way up the ladder to achieve important and responsible jobs as firemen, drivers, guards and station staff.

I suppose it is not surprising that a fair percentage of the friends from my teenage years, many of whom have remained lifelong pals, originally came together while pursuing their hobby on station footbridges or platforms, or when visiting our local engine shed at Fratton. Similarly, numerous elderly railway enthusiasts whose interest in railways began as humble trainspotters with a notebook and Biro in their hand are nowadays actively involved in some aspect of steam railway preservation.

My own personal trainspotting adventures have been well chronicled in the two published volumes of my *Diary of a Trainspotter* books, where complete lists of 'on shed' notings and observations and relevant photographs have been included. In contrast, *Forget the Anorak* sets out to provide an often amusing personal and social perspective from which to portray some of our silly antics. Nevertheless, its aim is to include *all* my treasured memories, and those of my fellow companions, minus the lists of 'on shed' locomotives – and to include the classic trips not only by rail but also by scooter and car when something 'unusual' always seemed to crop up.

When we were involved in trainspotting trips I don't think we ever thought that our lives might be in danger, especially when trudging the backstreets of Camden Town or Plaistow or similar locations in the West Midlands in search of some grimy, smoke-filled engine shed. Did we not realise the lurking dangers of dusk and night-time visits to dimly lit depots where our next step might prove fatal? We were oblivious to those kinds of danger, probably because we were teenagers, and teenagers in those days had precious little fear of anything or anyone. It was our determination to succeed in completing our scheduled timetables that spurred us on – we had set ourselves a target and would have felt defeated if it had not been fully achieved.

What a grand feeling and sense of achievement we humble trainspotters had as we totalled up our 'cops' on the homeward-bound train, knowing that we had successfully 'bunked' engine sheds crammed tight with living steam, eluded the foreman, made references and taken photographs (which in later years would become gems of nostalgia); and in addition to all this our travels always produced some very amusing stories. Our parents would always be somewhat anxious for our safe return, especially if we had been away for a weekend or a full week; my mum would welcome me home with a hot cup of tea and often with a generous slice of her home-made apple pie – it was then that I realised I was home.

1

Trainspotting, a Hobby

Trainspotting in its heyday between the mid-1950s and the late '60s was definitely a hobby suited to the outdoor, adventurous type of youth, someone full of boundless energy and not afraid to travel, sometimes hundreds of miles, with a night or nights away from the comforts of home. These could be spent in a station waiting-room or on an overnight train, or sometimes in the company of drunks or tramps on a hard wooden station seat more than likely exposed to all the elements.

My personal experiences included all these aspects of night-time trainspotting, not to mention sleeping rough on porters' trolleys amid the noise, steam and clanking movements of passing trains and engines, using only a plastic mac and cloth cap for cover and protection – and a cloth haversack as a pillow! I found the hobby a most fascinating one; while many of my schoolmates were roaming the streets of Portsmouth and Southsea in search of amusement, we trainspotters were often miles away travelling the railways of Great Britain and indulging in our adventurous hobby. It certainly kept us fully occupied, although with a few exceptions that will be revealed later.

There were of course other activities that kept the teenager of that era amused, including such diversions as stamp collecting, cigarette card collecting, *I Spy* books, the cinema, pop music and the inevitable encounters with the opposite sex!

The hobby of trainspotting inevitably involved a certain degree of risk, such as the illegal 'bunking' of British Railways engine sheds, workshops and other such installations. For us teenagers every trip undertaken was an adventure; sometimes we would acquire bogus permits or, more often, no permits at all, and these would be for engine shed visits miles away from our homes on trips that had been meticulously planned weeks ahead. I believe the non-existent paperwork added an air of excitement to many of our visits, and I think this is what helped to make the hobby both challenging and fulfilling.

Why did we on almost every trip inflict a rigorous, punishing, self-imposed time schedule on ourselves? It was, seemingly, only a harmless hobby but many of our non-railway pals and fellow schoolboys had the opinion that we were rather silly pursuing such a hobby, and it was common to hear such mundane remarks as 'What do you do when you've collected all the numbers?' or 'Once you've seen one, you've seen them all'. Little did they realise that in later years many of these trainspotters critically abused by their school pals would find employment courtesy of British Railways, and that after 1968, when this country decided to make steam-hauled trains extinct, these trainspotters would be found active in the field of steam preservation.

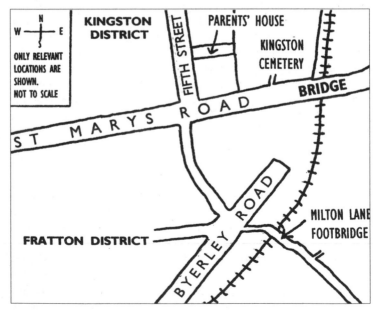

St Mary's Road bridge, my very first trainspotting location.

My First Glimpse

I recollect that I saw my very first British Railways steam locomotive of note, albeit from quite a distance, a 'King Arthur' class 4–6–0, when I was about twelve years old, living at that time with my mother and father in Fifth Street on the borders of the Kingston and Fratton districts of Portsmouth. Our house had a very long garden which included an apple tree and backed on to Kingston Cemetery. Beyond this area were the double-track main railway lines in and out of Portsmouth; when the trees were bare in the winter months I could plainly see the trains passing by from my bedroom window.

One of my treasured Christmas presents from my mum and dad was a shiny red scooter. I used this to investigate further my sightings of trains, as nearby St Mary's Road bridge was an ideal point from which to watch. Unfortunately, with the passage of time the very early lists of steam engine and electric unit numbers noted at this spot have been lost. Now, whenever I travel over St Mary's Road bridge, or more often than not travel under it by rail, it always brings back a tinge of nostalgia and rekindles my memory of first putting Biro to notebook and logging my first BR steam locomotive.

A Good Move

In the mid-1950s my parents decided to move from Fifth Street to Penhale Road in Fratton, a distance of approximately a mile and a half. This new district proved to be an excellent base from which to continue my interest in trains, since 'Sooty Footbridge' was just a matter of four or five minutes' walk away. This footbridge, nicknamed by the local railwaymen for obvious reasons, was accessible via a narrow side entrance in the middle of the densely populated terraced-house area of Byerley and Walmer roads – and being adjacent to the then Fratton East signal-box it led directly into the locomotive depot yard. Naturally, this means of entry was very tempting for us young trainspotters, but with the signal-box nearby and railway workers constantly using the bridge. I never personally attempted to enter this way – but that's not to say that some of my friends in later years were not successful. Sadly, the footbridge was demolished in the early 1960s and a few years later Fratton East signal-box suffered the same fate. Railway workers now had to enter the motive power depot via the main entrance in Goldsmith Avenue, a considerable distance away, especially if their homes were in the Fratton area.

About one hundred yards further north of Sooty Footbridge was, and still is, the location known as Milton Lane footbridge. This bridge comes alive whenever Portsmouth Football Club have a home fixture at the nearby Fratton Park; Milton Lane, a narrow pedestrian walkway, leads into what is known as Specks Lane and this in turn bounds the 'Milton End' of Fratton Park. Until the early 1960s there was on the northern side of the footbridge a sparsely used single-track branch line used only as a factories siding for the adjoining Rodney Road industrial estate. This line was no more than a few hundred yards in length, and when it was decided not to use it any more it became a siding for redundant wagons and eventually the track was lifted. The footbridge was not a very good location for photographs as it had a wire mesh all around, but nevertheless over the years I did obtain a few shots of trains from other angles on this bridge probably my most memorable being of 'S15' 4–6–0 No. 30839 in ex-works condition as it was hauling a freight out of Fratton goods yard.

Eddie Arrives on the Scene

Being an only child and having just moved house, I needed a friend or friends to share the early years of my trainspotting interest. It just so happened that my mother had many years previously attended the same school at Martha Street in central Portsmouth as a certain Ivy Rooke, and was joyously reunited with her soon after moving. Naturally I became friendly with her son Eddie, their house being ideally situated in Sandringham Road, the next road to ours. It turned out that Eddie also had a mild interest in railways and,

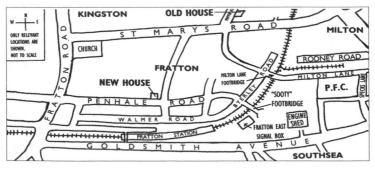

Map of Fratton and area showing my former and my new home.

although I did not know it at the time, this new-found friendship would become a lifelong partnership as we subsequently travelled by rail, scooter and car over the next fourteen years or so visiting countless engine sheds, workshops, scrapyards and stations all over Great Britain.

We enjoyed a tremendous variety of day, weekend and full-week trainspotting trips, and in later years the addition of a small tent gave rise to many an amusing story or anecdote, as you will find out later. Eddie and I were educated at separate schools and had our own sets of pals, but over a very short period of time Eddie and David Copus and his friends would soon become 'railway orientated', especially as the Southern Grammar School for Boys which Eddie attended had a popular 00 gauge model railway club. This was soon transformed into a thriving trainspotting club!

If my mother (her name was Edith Jane but she was always known as Cis) had not met up with Ivy Rooke and I in turn with her son, I wonder whether I would ever have continued my interest in railways from those very early days when I happily scootered to St Mary's Road bridge? Maybe I would have consigned myself to a pastime of fishing, cycling, aircraft-spotting, stamp-collecting or more than likely an interest in ships and the sea, as I did reside in a very famous naval port. I feel certain that whatever hobby may have constituted my lifelong interest it would have been considerably less interesting and no doubt a shade more boring. Looking back I could not imagine my life bereft of steam locomotives, group travelling, 'bunking' engine sheds and sleeping rough on railway stations – not forgetting those camping escapades and the great fun we derived from each and every trip undertaken, no matter what the mode of transport.

Had it not been for my interest in trains and Eddie's appearance on the scene, I am sure I wouldn't have travelled to all those towns and cities throughout Great Britain by any other means of transport, as neither my mum nor my dad had a car and had never driven a vehicle in their lives. I actually passed my driving test in 1968 in a Ford Anglia, but by this date the demise of British Railways steam power was virtually complete and I just could not face motoring around the country in search of diesels, multiple units and electric trains. To me they were lifeless and could not compare with a steam locomotive, a piece of live machinery breathing steam. I never took up the challenge of driving.

It's all in the past now – and that is what this book is all about, all those incidents that inevitably occurred whenever a trainspotting trip was undertaken all those years ago. No one really wants to look too far into the future as it is scary and unpredictable; we will probably be best remembered by being labelled as 'anoraks', and the jokes about that word have really got a bit beyond their sell-by date. Anyway, we never wore anoraks – they didn't become popular until the diesel age and that was another era.

We trainspotters, always harping on about the past and trying to relive old memories, are probably looked upon in today's high-tech world as a collection of boring old farts, completely sexless, like stone statues standing at the end of busy railway station platforms oblivious to everything else around them. Let people think what they like – I see it in a different light. Nothing could be further from the truth. The majority of my railway enthusiast friends were very learned people both from grammar and secondary school education, who went on to hold important jobs – as employees of British Rail, as bankers, printers, caterers and office staff and as part of our local work-force of skilled craftsmen in the Royal Naval Dockyard in Portsmouth.

Be that as it may, it was the arrival of Eddie Rooke on the scene in the mid-1950s that provided a stepping-stone that enabled me to progress further with my early railway observations.

2

The Focal Point

It was only a ten-minute walk from Penhale Road to my local railway station of Fratton (built in 1885), the footbridge of which would become a focal point for railway enthusiasts and trainspotters both young and old; this ideal location remained a very popular meeting place right up to the demise of Southern Region steam-hauled trains in July 1967. In those years the footbridge was smartly painted in the SR colours of green and cream and it possessed a complete roof. Naturally, its windows were nearly always grimy and smoke-stained, especially those just above the three main- line railway tracks. I discovered at a later date that the ironwork used in the construction of the footbridge was shipped in from America.

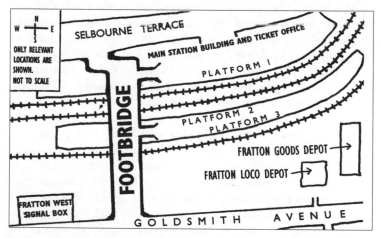

Fratton station footbridge was an ideal meeting base for local trainspotters.

Adjacent to the footbridge and backing on to the brick wall in Goldsmith Avenue was Fratton West signal-box, sadly now demolished – the scars still remain to this day.

Many happy hours were idled away on the footbridge, as there was always a tremendous variety of both SR electric units and steam locomotive classes to be seen. For us 'Portmuthians' the direct line from London (Waterloo) had been electrified by the addition of a third rail in 1937 and electric units were part of the everyday scene. Sometimes we strained through binoculars to pick out the numbers of steam locomotives lined up in the distant Fratton depot yard and passed on details to our companions on the bridge. Beyond the depot and clearly visible from the footbridge was the unmistakable zigzag design of the roof of Fratton goods depot.

From the mid-1950s I had the use of my father's Brownie box camera. I took most photographs in and around Fratton station and the nearby locomotive depot, but I gradually built up a collection from other local viewpoints. Over the years the camera was taken on SR and WR Rail Rovers and countless other trainspotting trips all over Great Britain. My dad paid the sum of 27s 6d when he purchased it in 1926. At the time this would have been quite a considerable sum of money and the camera was probably a luxury he saved up to purchase. I am very glad that he allowed me the use of it – and this camera is still with me and in working order to this day.

As a result of meeting other trainspotters on the footbridge, and our consequent sharing of railway information and discussion of trips and excursions, Eddie and I were tempted to make some speculative and grand plans to visit other stations, engine sheds and workshops all over the railway system between the mid-1950s and the end of BR steam in August 1968. Following the introduction of Sunday Excursion trains from Portsmouth Harbour station and Portsmouth Football Club away trip 'Specials', we obviously capitalised on the new accessibility of cities and towns which we would otherwise never have visited – especially since such trips cost only a cheap return fare, whereas some of our other trainspotting trips were undertaken on ordinary day return tickets. That would change when we began to use other types of tickets such as 'group' or 'workman's' that gave us considerable fare reductions. An added bonus was that our travels around Britain increased our knowledge not only of the rail network but also of areas of geographical and industrial interest.

My very first engine shed visit was with Eddie Rooke to Eastleigh depot (71A), even before I had attempted my local depot of Fratton. The date will always stick in my mind – Wednesday 24 August 1955, during the summer holidays – and it started a trend that continued for a further thirteen years: the depot was 'bunked'! I can still recall the smoke-filled panorama of the straight shed and yards tightly crammed with eighty-six steam engines, of which forty-three were main-line types. And to note no fewer than twenty-one Bulleid 4–6–2s in one swoop was pure bliss. We did not look back – our railway shed visits had begun and we wanted more!

Fratton station footbridge on a summer Saturday or Sunday was a guaranteed hive of activity. Apart from the usual SR electric unit trains to and from Waterloo, Victoria, Brighton and Chichester, there were the steam-hauled trains to and from Cardiff General, Bristol, Eastleigh, Southampton and Andover Junction, and the occasional working to Waterloo via Eastleigh and Basingstoke. In addition to these service trains one could expect to see holiday excursions from the Midlands or North London areas. In those days a factory would close its doors completely for two weeks, and its employees had the option of a special seaside excursion train laid on for them to 'Sunny Southsea', as the local brochure described our area. I am sure that most factory workers and staff took full advantage of this offer. Western Region classes would be widely used on these trains, the most common being the 'Hall' class 4–6–0s with their gleaming brass fittings and intriguing name-plates.

It was very satisfying for us local trainspotters to help passengers take their holiday luggage and heavy suitcases and bags up the steps from platforms 2 and 3. Sometimes we carried the luggage to a waiting taxi or to Platform 1 and usually – and joyfully – received a sixpenny tip for our efforts. The station staff obviously did not mind us performing these duties as it saved them the bother of having to push the luggage on trolleys across the double tracks at the Portsmouth end of the station platform.

Fratton engine shed could be viewed from the footbridge, but it was some distance away. The building was unique in being the only Southern Region depot with a complete roundhouse. In the mid-1950s its allocation of locomotives amounted to twenty-eight and it had the distinction of never having a diesel in its allocation, although several 0–6–0 shunters from Eastleigh could be found on shunting duties in the adjacent goods yards. Without a doubt the most loved engines at my local depot were the diminutive 'AIX' class 0–6–0 tanks affectionately known as 'Hayling Billy' engines because they were used on the nearby Havant to Hayling Island branch line.

Travels Widen

It was during the summer holidays of 1956 that at the tender age of fifteen I and a selection of my trainspotting pals from the station footbridge started our railway station and engine shed visits in earnest. We began by purchasing half-fare day return tickets to places not too distant such as London, Westbury, Salisbury, Swindon and Brighton and, at the start of the following year, took advantage of the popular Sunday Excursions that were laid on to such far-flung destinations as Wolverhampton and Cardiff. This was when my trainspotting hobby really got moving.

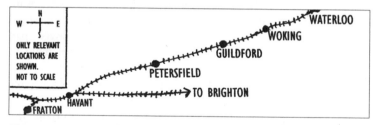

This was our route on the Workman's train from Fratton to Waterloo via Petersfield.

A journey to London with its array of engine sheds, such as Camden, Cricklewood, Old Oak Common, Willesden and Neasden, and its famous terminus stations was always something special. To obtain the maximum number of hours in the capital our happy band of teenagers would depart from Fratton station at the unearthly hour of 5.32 a.m., on what was known as the 'workman's' train!

This train would normally be a green-liveried Southern Region '2-BIL' electric unit comprising four two-carriage units and displaying a '7' headcode. Tickets had to be purchased in two separate stages. The first was Fratton to Petersfield, costing about 6s. On arrival at Petersfield, where a stop of five minutes was scheduled, one of our group would dash out of the train to the ticket office via the subway and buy the required number of Workman's return tickets to Waterloo. In the late 1950s this would set us back about 8s. The complete return journey would cost us in the region of 14s. Unfortunately, the only drawback with this type of ticket was that the train would stop to pick up workmen at virtually every station and halt between Fratton and Waterloo – eventually arriving at 7.48 a.m.!

Of course, a workman's ticket was not available on a Sunday, so on these occasions we purchased half-fare day return tickets departing on the 6.08 a.m. all-stations electric unit train from Fratton. The compensation for the additional fare and later departure was to be able to visit the engine sheds and see them packed tight with simmering steam, the majority of the locomotives resting and awaiting their respective duties for the forthcoming week. Engineering work on British Railways tracks was usually carried out only on Sundays if I recall correctly; very few major track-

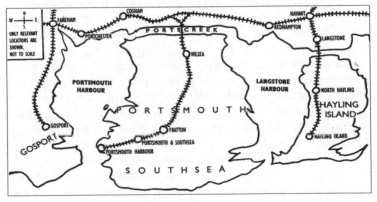

Portsmouth and neighbouring Gosport and Hayling Island. The narrow strip of water known as Portscreek is clearly shown – making Portsmouth an island.

repair jobs were undertaken on a Saturday or during the week. The experience of travelling by replacement double-decker bus from Fratton station approach to Havant on a Sunday morning because of local engineering work is one of my abiding memories, especially as the train guard also travelled on the bus and felt it his duty to blow a very loud blast on his whistle to set the bus on its way!

Portsea Island, on Foot and by Bike

One of our favourite pastimes when we were free from the clutches of trainspotting and visits to see 'Pompey' at Fratton Park was to take a lengthy walk around various districts of Portsmouth and its seaside resort of Southsea. This could be anything up to a distance of 8 miles, nearly always in groups of six or more, and it provided us teenagers with some ideal exercise in preparation for the forthcoming punishing schedule which we always seemed to have set ourselves. I refer to our next trainspotting trip of course.

As the city of Portsmouth is relatively flat, walking and cycling are quite effortless. In fact Portsmouth is an island (many people living outside the area are unaware of this) as it is separated from the mainland by a very narrow strip of water known as Portscreek. Portsmouth was originally known as Portsea Island, and covers an area approximately 6 miles from north to south and 4 miles from east to west. Today it has a population of nearly 190,000.

During our walks we would inevitably stop off at a café for Coca-Cola or a milkshake, and if we were in the vicinity of Verrecchia's Ice Cream Parlour we would indulge in an appetising knickerbocker glory or maybe just a cup of coffee. It was while taking a break at one of these coffee shops that our group would formulate plans for engine shed visits on our next daytrip or maybe Sunday excursion. David Copus, a very close friend, not only came on virtually every railway trip but also accompanied us on these lengthy walks and always brought with him *The British Railways Locomotive Shed Directory*. This would be consulted while we consumed our drinks and plans would be drawn up for the order of locomotive depot visits. David was also the 'main man' when it came to sending off for official permits to visit these installations. However, after receiving initial permits over a period of time for visits over a wide area of England and Wales, a slight 'amendment' date-wise was made for future use – more about that later!

I bought my very first bicycle in the early 1960s; it was a brand new Raleigh 'New Yorker', a shiny, red, three-speed bike that cost £25 from Allen's in Albert Road, Southsea. My new-found pedal power proved to be a most convenient means of transport, not only for work in Blackfriars Road, Southsea, but also in taking me to places such as Fratton station, the engine shed and David Copus's house, which was ideally situated just opposite the engine shed main gate. At this date Eddie and many of our companions had also taken up cycling.

Once a week my bike came in useful in helping to carry my mother's shopping from the large Co-op store in Fratton Road. In those days there were countless shops in Fratton Road from which you could choose to make up your weekly shopping list. I recall the Home and Colonial Stores, Pink's the grocers and Timothy White's – the latter being situated on the corner of Arundel Street and Fratton Road – but my favourite shop was a marvellous toy shop by the name of Evelyn's. This was where my parents purchased my first real train set – a large black-liveried 'Princess Royal' class 4–6–2 engine, carrying a red name-plate, *Princess Elizabeth*, with a set of accessories that included a set of 'blood and custard' carriages, a circle of 00-gauge track and a control box. I vaguely remember my parents buying me a tin clockwork 0–4–0 engine with some track and assorted wagons at some time before this, but with the passage of time it has unfortunately been lost.

Cycling around Portsmouth in the 1960s was a pleasure without the volume of cars and heavy vehicles on the roads which we have to endure today. People who worked in the Royal Naval Dockyard almost always used pedal power to get there. The sight of hundreds of 'Dockies' emerging from Unicorn Gate at least ten abreast on their way to dinner break, and repeated in the late afternoon when they went home, is something I shall never forget. They cycled in hordes up Edinburgh Road before gradually dispersing into the Arundel Street and Commercial Road area. While on the subject of the dockyard, it is worth mentioning that no less than 25 miles of standard-gauge railway track once existed within its walls. Over sixty steam locomotives and a handful of diesels were used during its lifetime. They had their own engine shed, and repairs were carried out within the dockyard. All this activity was on our doorstep, yet we local trainspotters were kept away by guarded gates.

In the summer months especially, Eddie Rooke would quite often cycle 23 miles to visit or 'bunk' Eastleigh depot (71A). Sometimes, if he was lucky or had previously planned it, he would meet up with a group of touring railway enthusiasts, usually some obscure railway club or society from the Midlands or the north east of England; he would then tag on to the group and gain admittance to Eastleigh Locomotive Works in Campbell Road.

Early in the 1960s I found that cycling could get me to some of the lesser-known locations along the railway lines in Portsmouth. With my dad's box camera safely packed in the saddle-bag, I would cycle to such line-side points as Copnor bridge, Kingston Cemetery, Moneyfields Lane bridge and Green Lane Crossing to capture photographs of the passing trains. These cycling experiences were mainly confined to Portsea Island, with occasional visits to Southsea, Eastney, Copnor and Hilsea, the latter two also offering some additional railway photographic viewpoints. Hayling Island would be visited in the summer months, usually via the small ferry from Eastney. Gosport, on the western side of Portsmouth Harbour, was reached by ferry from Portsmouth Harbour.

Six and a Quarter Miles

In the 1950s and 1960s the 6¼ miles of railway between Fratton and Havant were always full of interest for the railway enthusiast. As you departed from Platform 1 and headed round the left-hand curve you would first catch a glimpse on the right of the sizeable water tower and the steam locomotives lined up in Fratton depot yard. Classes would vary considerably but you could nearly always note a 'U' class 2–6–0, a 'T9' class 4–4–0, a 'C2X' class 0–6–0 or a 'Standard', and tucked away next to the coaling crane DS200 would be an 'A1X' class 0–6–0 tank which was used on the Havant to Hayling Island branch.

Also on the right you would pass Fratton East signal-box, then Sooty footbridge, followed closely by Milton Lane footbridge. The extensive goods sidings led off from Milton Lane footbridge to the goods depot building, one of the largest in Great Britain, conspicuous by virtue of its zigzag roof. In this area one would nearly always see some shunting in progress, being carried out mostly by Fratton's three 'E4' class 0–6–2 tanks, numbers 32479, 32495 and 32509. Occasionally an 0–6–0 diesel shunter from Eastleigh would be lurking in the vicinity. Adjacent to the goods depot one could clearly see the home ground of our beloved Portsmouth Football Club, Fratton Park (opened 1898). Immediately after Milton Lane footbridge was St Marys General Hospital, where a very tall concrete chimney with a distinctive bulge in the centre was partially visible.

Moving on, you would pass Kingston Recreation Ground on the left, then go under St Mary's Road bridge with Kingston

Cemetery on your left and HM Kingston Prison on the right before passing under Copnor Road bridge. Almost hidden away as you approached the bridge was the former cottage of a long-gone level-crossing; this small building had a thriving garden where in the summer months you could see runner beans, potatoes, tomatoes and lettuce growing in abundance. Next came Moneyfields Lane footbridge, but owing to the expansion of factories in this area, Burrfields Road bridge was constructed in the mid-1960s.

Next along the line was Green Lane crossing and signal-box and to the right were the enormous cylinders known as Hilsea Gas Works, where there was a network of railway tracks that included a single-line engine shed next to the main line. If you were lucky or quick enough you might see one of several saddle-tank steam locomotives either at work or tucked away inside the shed. Fratton-allocated 'E1' class 0–6–0 tanks also frequented these sidings. In later years, I recall, Hilsea Gas Works had a bright-red-liveried 0–6–0 diesel shunter which was named *Fleet No. 1139*. Also at this location was an Andrew Barclay 0–4–0 saddle-tank, *Lord Fisher*, built in 1915. It was resident for many years before finding a new home at Cranmore on the East Somerset Railway.

Having passed the gas works the next notable location was on the left before Hilsea Halt: the former Royal Ordnance sidings led off from the Up line to terminate near Peronne Road at some sizeable corrugated buildings, which are still *in situ* today although the tracks and platforms have long since disappeared. Hilsea Halt (1941) was built to cater for the then thriving Portsmouth City Airport and the extensive industrial estate nearby. From March 1959 until its demolition, which I think occurred in the 1970s, the station boasted a very impressive-looking Callender-Hamilton footbridge at its north end. This structure had originally been sited on the north side of the Cosham triangle, and was relocated at Hilsea to relieve congestion at what was then named Rat Lane, known today as Norway Road – its use was only intended for pedestrians and cyclists.

Leaving Hilsea Halt you would pass through a very short tunnel at a point where the defences of Portsmouth had to be breached in 1847 to allow the railway to enter Portsea Island. Once Portscreek had been crossed you caught a glimpse of the adjacent signal-box on the edge of the water, and the train took the eastern side of the Cosham triangle. Immediately on the left were the three

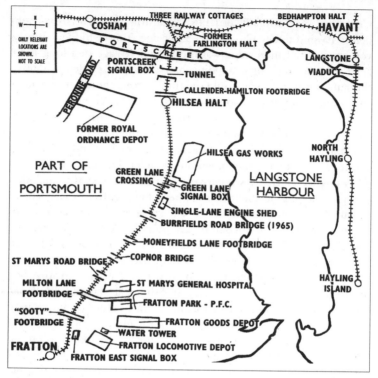

The 6¼ miles between Fratton and Havant were always full of interest for the railway enthusiast.

white-washed railway cottages, still inhabited today. In those days the railway triangle was open; cattle grazed freely there, and it also possessed quite a sizeable pond. Next was the former site of Farlington Halt, which for many years had catered for an adjoining racecourse. It was near this point that we trainspotters would be looking out of the window in the hope of seeing a steam-hauled freight or more often than not a passenger train on the north side of the triangle. This passenger train would be waiting at signals for our train to pass and we were often rewarded with the sight of an 'H2' class 4–4–2 on a train heading for Brighton; I remember seeing No. 32424 *Beachy Head* at this location. In later years 'West Country' and 'Battle of Britain' 4–6–2s were frequently used on this line – they would have started off from either Plymouth or Cardiff, bound for Brighton.

Although not indicated on the accompanying map, there were other interesting locations on the section of line between the Cosham triangle and Havant. On the north side of the triangle were the Co-op sidings serving the dairy buildings. On the right, approaching Bedhampton Halt, were at one time sidings leading to a flour mill, with a level-crossing behind Bidbury Mead. It was in this area that my pal, David Copus, was employed at Portsmouth Water Company. A short distance west of Havant station was Stockheath level-crossing.

Bedhampton Halt (1906) was passed next and from there it was a short journey to the quite large and spread-out station at Havant (1859). Here we would be looking out for a 'A1X' class 0–6–0 tank engine either arriving, taking water or awaiting departure from the bay platform on the Down side of the main line. A handful of these diminutive tanks were specially allocated to Fratton depot to work the 4½ mile Havant to Hayling Island branch. They were much loved not only by the drivers and firemen but also by the general public, and became affectionately known as 'Hayling Billy' engines. Unfortunately, Dr Beeching's axe fell on the line in 1963, when the Railway Inspectorate declared that the wooden viaduct crossing Langstone Harbour was unsafe. Ironically, it took three charges of high explosives to make it budge and the concrete supports are still there today – I think that tells us a story!

These 6¼ miles from Fratton were packed full of interest for a railway enthusiast in those days, something about which modern trainspotters can only dream.

3

My 'Other World'

When I was sixteen and attending Kingston Modern School for Boys in Olinda Street, Portsmouth, I was totally unaware that in December that year, 1956, I would have to leave school and earn a living. In fact it was only during the last few months of my school career that it dawned on me I would be going out into the wide world. I was quite proud of how I had performed my duties as a school prefect. In my final year under strict form master Mr Evans, I came second in a class of thirty-six in my favourite subject, English, and was also second in Art and third in Geography. The headmaster, Mr R.R. Davies, encouraged my employment hopes in his comment on my 'End of Session' school report which stated: 'Michael's school career has been highly commendable.' That is not to say that I never misbehaved, especially in my earlier school days. I did get into trouble, like most boys, which inevitably resulted in being sent to the headmaster's room where the dreaded cane was felt on the backside. To combat this discomfort, we would first visit the cloakroom and carefully insert a folded school scarf down the back of our trousers – it certainly helped to soften the blows!

I applied first for a shipwright's job in Portsmouth Royal Naval Dockyard but there were no vacancies. Undaunted, I next visited Fratton locomotive depot to speak to the foreman, a Mr Butler, about a job as an engine driver. I took a medical examination at Eastleigh but unfortunately one of my eyes was weak and I was rejected. Then I met up with a school pal, David Wills, who told me a few basic points about the trade that he had just taken up. This roused my interest and within a few weeks I had secured a job as an apprentice hot-metal compositor at the Grosvenor Press printing works in Blackfriars Road, Southsea. It was a 15-minute walk from my parents' house in Penhale Road, Fratton and my starting wage was £2 14s 6d, the equivalent of about £40 today. I worked from 8 a.m. to 6 p.m. Monday to Friday with an hour's dinner break. Needless to say, as the works was only two minutes walk from 'Jacob's Ladder' – the nickname of the footbridge spanning the railway tracks on the approach to Portsmouth and Southsea station – I had some time to trainspot after returning from dinner.

Monday 7 January 1957, my first day of employment, was the beginning of virtually a lifelong association with Grosvenor Press. It lasted almost thirty-seven years until August 1993 – when the few members of the work force and staff were all made redundant.

Going to work in the morning, firstly on foot and later by bike, had its advantages in that I would use the route via Fratton Bridge, Canal Walk and Somers Road bridge, at which point I would stop and gaze down into the former canal basin area to get a look at the small tank engine waiting at the signal gantry with a goods train. This train would be bound for the dockyard and for many years it had my favourite Fratton engine hauling the wagons and vans, 'E1' class 0–6–0 tank No. 32694. It started off from Fratton goods yard on a twice-a-day trip and the train had to work 'wrong line' off Portsmouth and Southsea (High Level) station to gain admittance to the single track to the Royal Naval Dockyard.

This 'turn' was also worked by 'O2' class 0–4–4 tank engine No. 30207, other Fratton-allocated 'E1' class 0 6 0s Nos 32138 and 32139, and in later years 'U' class 2–6–0s, a selection of Standard

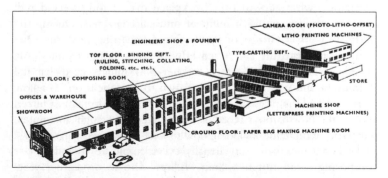

The printing works of Grosvenor Press, Blackfriars Road, Southsea.

class 4 2–6–0s and 2–6–4 tanks and even a Western Region pannier tank. Eastleigh provided an 0–6–0 diesel shunter in the mid-1960s. No. 32694 was used until its transfer to Southampton Docks depot (71I) in December 1960 and it was eventually sent to Eastleigh Works for scrapping in mid-1961.

In 1965 the Blackfriars Road printing factory (built in 1923) was demolished to make way for high-rise flats and new roads. Its associate company, Hampshire Paper Bag Manufacturing Company Limited, in nearby Middle Street, was closed at a later date and Grosvenor Press was then relocated to the Cosham area of Portsmouth. In November 1965 I moved to a new, purpose-built printing works in Northarbour Road, where I would accumulate nineteen years of double-day shift working. Again, many of my shift breaks here were happily spent trainspotting, as the factory conveniently backed onto the double track between Cosham and Portchester. An added incentive in the autumn months was the abundance of blackberry bushes – many a day I had my Tupperware lunch box filled to bursting point!

Purpose-built or not, the design of the factory left a lot to be desired. I worked in a large composing room where daylight was essential but we had no windows; the roof was a flat design and was leak-prone and over the years there was constant rainwater penetration – not an ideal situation for a printing works where paper was stored! On a different level, the top floor would have ideally suited the composing department as it had large full-length windows, but this was for office and staff use only; the canteen also had large windows – clearly a misjudgement by the planners!

Anyone who stays in one workplace over a long period will become familiar with a handful of unusual characters. During my thirty-six years at Grosvenor Press I found this to be very true. One former workmate, the late Alfred Edward Irish, springs to mind. Alf, or Alfie as he was known, was a Cockney-born midget-sized chap full of humour and wit, which he often used to play tricks on his fellow workers. I had the pleasure of being 'under his wing' for almost fifteen years at the Northarbour Road printing factory. He taught me quite a few tricks of the trade, including how to look busy when you're not!

Alf had a nickname for virtually every employee, including our composing room foreman, Stan Phillips, who in my earlier years at the Blackfriars Road printing factory was a most difficult man to please and often had me in tears. All that changed when Alf came along. Stan always wore a white coat, was as miserable as sin, sported a lovely shiny dome and dashed around the composing room at great speed – he was thus known as the 'White Tornado'! When Stan got annoyed with Alf for some reason, Alf's reply would be something like 'Keep your hair on, Stan!' A certain Chris Capon was inevitably nicknamed 'the Chicken', while a tall skinny lad by the name of Thornton was christened 'Skelly'.

I am a Silent Salesman
I would like to go to bed with you tonight
If the answer is YES, keep this card.
If the answer is NO, please return it,
as I am running out of cards.

Here are just two of the numerous joke cards that were the brainchild of Alf Irish.

POLITE NOTICE
our aim is to keep this place clean -
YOUR AIM WILL HELP

GENTLEMEN: Stand close, it may be shorter than you think.
LADIES: Please remain seated during the whole performance.

One of Alf's pranks was to tell me that Stan Phillips would be performing a 'Sand Dance' in his office. At first I was quite mystified but what he meant soon became clear after I discovered that he had sprinkled a handful of sugar on the office floor! The setting up by hand and printing of illegal jobs included business cards, joke cards and even posters; in the printing trade these were commonly known as 'Rabbits'. Alf was no exception, and a whole host of amusing joke cards and poems emerged from the 'Yampy Room' – this was the nickname given to the room where both Alf and I worked on examination papers. A notice above the door read 'You don't have to be mad to work here, but it helps!'

In his later years Alf's wit and humour were coupled to a cunning plan to earn some additional income. When the office staff sent round a slip of paper to check on dates of birth and other relative details, Alf altered the year of his date of birth.

His workmates seemed rather puzzled as to why he suddenly decided to work virtually every Saturday and Sunday on overtime for almost three years. Then someone in the office twigged and realised that Alf Irish was nearly sixty-eight years old – three years past his official retirement age!

While at Grosvenor Press I became actively involved in the running of the Sports and Social Club, being wholly dedicated to my duties and enjoying what I was doing for the pleasure of others. The 'railway connection' continued since in my capacity first as a committee member and then as secretary I promoted via the works notice-boards what were known as the British Rail Awayday 'Pleasure Seeker' excursions. I would make a block booking for our club of up to twenty people on these trips. We went to such places as Wroxham (Norfolk) to visit the Bressingham Gardens and Live Steam Museum (£3.50 return), Blackpool Illuminations (£3.25 return) and Cardiff and Barry Island (£3.00 return), all in the mid-1970s.

4

Encounters of the Other Kind

If I remember correctly, my first encounter with the opposite sex came when I was attending George Street School for Boys and Girls in the Kingston area of Portsmouth in the mid-1950s. I had taken a fancy to a rather tall girl from the same school, Jennifer Knight, who had blue eyes and long blonde hair. We met after school at her parents' house in Aylesbury Road opposite the school, and played pop records on her battery-operated record-player. The friendship fell apart when my parents moved house to Fratton and I lost contact with her.

As most of my trainspotting friends lived in the Fratton, Milton, Eastney and Southsea areas of Portsmouth, Eddie Rooke and I decided to join the Devonshire Avenue Youth Club, which was attached to the church and located on the corner of Winter Road and Devonshire Avenue in Southsea.

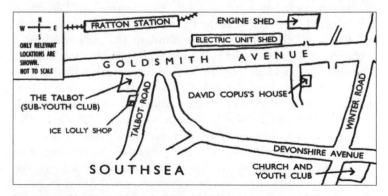

Locations of both youth clubs attended, together with other relevant locations mentioned in this chapter.

Our intention in joining this club was to chat up the girls who went there and ask them out — maybe to the cinema, or a pop concert at the Guildhall or possibly the Savoy on Southsea sea front where live rock and roll bands performed. The rules of the club stated that members should try to attend the Sunday evening church service whenever possible. We did manage this at the outset but as the months wore on the church attendances seemed to fade away and girls were the main attraction. Looking back over our early years at this youth club it is hard to believe that we abused the facilities when attending the church services, but as a group of young boys we were always looking for fun, even during a service. One highlight of the Sunday evening service would be when the word 'throne' occurred in a hymn — this was one of our silly words for a toilet and whenever it appeared there would be some fits of suppressed laughter and maybe some giggling between David Copus and another half-dozen of our mates in the back row! One Sunday evening when the sermon was particularly boring, a pack of playing cards was produced and very discreetly our back row contrived to play 'Snap'. All went well until someone dropped the pack of cards, scattering them all over the floor. We just had time to retrieve them before the vicar came round to shake hands with us at the end of the service.

One Saturday evening at the youth club will stick in my mind forever as an incident took place which proved to be a talking point for many a year. I was in the company of the usual companions and playing a game of darts, when I was apparently distracted by the passing by of a girl in a very short mini-skirt. Forgetting briefly that I was playing darts, I turned round for a closer view and promptly dispatched the dart through the glass window! I explained to the club leader that I had slipped and lost my balance! Through this incident our group became friends with the girl concerned and in turn she introduced her friends to us, meeting at such locations as Verrecchia's Ice Cream Parlour in the Guildhall Square or Delmonico's Coffee Lounge in Southsea. Whenever we met, the darts incident nearly always came up in conversation.

To combine trainspotting and the pursuit of the fairer sex was almost out of the question, but we did manage to achieve the unlikely combination on summer Saturdays and Sundays when meeting on Fratton station footbridge to note the excursions and holiday specials arriving from the Midlands. We would quickly, between arrivals, pop round the corner to Talbot Road and visit the small general store, from where we purchased great numbers of ice lollies; we always made sure that we were served by the shop owner's daughter, a very well-endowed young lady with red hair! Needless to say, we all fancied her, and she must have realised this as we made countless visits during the day. I don't think we ever attempted to chat her up, but you can imagine that the profits from the ice lollies we bought were substantial! It's worth mentioning that these ice lollies sold at one or two pennies each and they were shop-made – not mass-produced as today.

Girlfriends were never a long-term arrangement in those early years. In fact, none of our group of boys ever wanted this as railways, steam locomotives, football and music – probably in that order – came before any serious relationship with girls ever entered our minds. Nevertheless, they did arrive on the scene but were kept completely separate from trainspotting, which was our life. The youth club continued and we met up with more girls. David Copus appeared to be the sole member of our group who detested girls; and it gave us a platform to wind him up on numerous occasions. We would send girls round to his parents' house late on a Friday or Saturday evening telling them that there was a party at that address and that they were invited. Of course there was no such thing and David, realising it was the work of his close pals, turned a blind eye to our antics – a few words were usually spoken when we next met but in the main we remained the best of mates.

Intimate relationships with girls were very few and far between, and when we did 'score' a purchase from the chemists or 'something for the weekend' after a visit to the hairdressers (dome-scraping constabulary) was looked upon as great fun!

I vividly remember Saturday 4 July 1964, as it was then that Eddie Rooke, David Copus, Tony Ingram, Frank Allen, Barry Dyer and I travelled to London on the electric unit train from Fratton. We had obtained tickets for a rock and roll concert in the Royal Albert Hall but did not realise until our arrival that our seats were way up in the gods. This, however, would bring us some compensation via the fairer sex. The concert is probably most remembered because the star performer, P.J. Proby, had the misfortune to split his trousers during his stage act – this resulted in hordes of screaming teenage girls leaping onto the stage! Included in that memorable concert were other top artists such as the Crickets and the Applejacks, along with a host of lesser-known acts.

That night we had the good fortune to meet six girls who were seated near us. After the concert was finished they told us that they were planning to stay overnight in a hostel near the British Air Terminal in Cromwell Road, West London. If my memory is correct we all travelled from the concert by bus, six youths and six girls. While on this journey we decided we would all spend the night on long comfortable cushioned seats in the British Air Terminal! Barry Dyer's claim to fame that night was that he had a six-hour snogging session! As David Copus was anti-female, we made sure that he got the 'grotty' one! Believe it or not, that night we all experienced a reasonable night's kip. One of my pals, Tony Ingram, obviously had a lasting effect on the young lady he had met. We learnt at a later date that he had travelled the considerable distance to Blackpool to meet her again!

Before our arrival at the Royal Albert Hall we had obviously, as trainspotters, indulged in visits to the terminus railway stations at Charing Cross, Euston and Paddington using the tube and buses for transport and it was at some point in these travels that we came upon a small chemists shop. There we severely embarrassed a young female assistant: in turn we each entered the shop and asked her in a very deep voice, 'Can I have a packet of three, please?' I was the final customer and by this time her face was as red as a beetroot! Those packets, needless to say, remained unopened that night!

The Sub Youth Club was in a large room above the Talbot Hotel (an impressive Cogswell-designed timbered structure) which still stands on the corner of Talbot Road and Goldsmith Avenue, though it is no longer a public house. This venue was used whenever the Devonshire Avenue Youth Club hall had other functions booked. For us trainspotters, it gave us not only a grandstand view of railway movements through the adjacent Fratton station during the summer months, but also the chance to bring along a selection of our own 45rpm pop singles to play on the club's record-player – and, obviously, to try to impress the girls present!

5

A Bygone Age on our Doorstep

Ryde, on the Isle of Wight, or the 'Garden Isle' as it is known, is located roughly 5 sea miles from Portsmouth Harbour on the mainland, yet in the 1950s and '60s we trainspotters rarely ventured across Spithead on the thirty-minute ferry trip. Even in 1965 when the world's first commercial hovercraft service plied between Clarence Pier (Southsea) and Ryde, taking a mere ten minutes, it did not tempt us to make more visits to the island. We should have been drooling over the remaining handful of steam-operated passenger services on the island, whose days by now were numbered.

If we did visit the Isle of Wight, it was not often and usually in the company of our parents, although Eddie Rooke had made several forays in the summer months to play cricket for his school. Visits with my parents took in some superb scenery, quaint villages and stunning coastlines – we would travel by both train and bus. But for me and a few of my trainspotting friends the main attraction was the O2 class 0–4–4 steam locomotives, those tank engines of 1923 vintage that operated on what was once an extensive island railway network. Apart from these engines, there were vintage carriages, original station buildings, signal-boxes and semaphore signals – which all seemed to have 'stood still with time'. Here we found solace in an idyllic setting in which a railway operated virtually unchanged from a bygone age.

The annual summer visit to the island became one of my parents' rituals; I was included and my memories stretch as far back as far as I can go! We would always take a 'Round the Island' coach tour on arriving at Ryde, but on other occasions a ride behind an 'O2' class to such locations as Newport, Cowes, Sandown, Shanklin and Ventnor was sampled with great enthusiasm. I never did get to travel by rail to Bembridge, Ventnor West, Yarmouth or Freshwater, as all these lines were axed in the early 1950s. Anyway, on the lines that we did travel I frequently took the opportunity not only to photograph but also to tape record some of the locomotives and their sounds. On many occasions we would alight from the train at Ryde St Johns Road station, and I would send my parents into a nearby public house for several glasses of Mackeson while I 'bunked' the adjacent Ryde depot (70H)!

My sole recollection of being accompanied by a fellow trainspotter is one Sunday in April 1958. David Bodenham and I caught the PS *Ryde* from Portsmouth Harbour (adjacent to the station) and decided on a 'triple bunk' of Ryde depot, Ryde Works and Newport depot (70G). Although Newport had closed in late 1957, four 'O2' class tanks were stored inside the depot 'out of use'. Our trip was an attempt to note *all* nineteen 'O2' class tanks and the two remaining 1874-vintage 'E1' class 0–6–0 tanks Nos 3, *Ryde* and 4, *Wroxall*. On that particular Sunday railway officials appeared to be non-existent, and the few that we did encounter

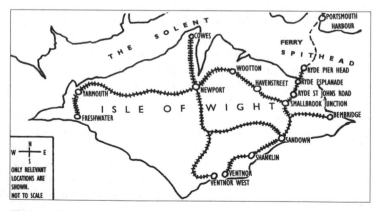

This map shows the once extensive network of railways on the Isle of Wight. Sadly today all that remains is the Ryde Pier Head to Shanklin section, while the Isle of Wight Steam Railway operates vintage steam trains between Smallbrook Junction and Wootton.

turned a blind eye to our presence. Needless to say, we successfully completed all three 'bunkings', noting the complete Isle of Wight allocation of twenty-one steam locomotives.

My passion for the Isle of Wight, not only for its vintage railway locomotives, but also for its breathtaking scenery, led me in the late 1960s to become a member of the Wight Locomotive Society. I made weekend visits to the closed Newport station, where I did my bit along with other society members in helping to restore one of the ex-SR vintage green-liveried carriages. In the summer months a complete weekend would be spent at Newport, overnight accommodation being courtesy of one of the carriages.

Whenever I visit the Isle of Wight today, a ride on the section of track between Smallbrook Junction and Wootton via Havenstreet is a 'must'. This is now the only remaining steam-hauled section, operated by the Isle of Wight Steam Railway and run by a bunch of extremely dedicated volunteers amid typical island scenery. Havenstreet station, the adjacent engine shed and workshops, together with an excellent museum and bookshop and other facilities, cannot be missed. The area really comes alive every August Bank Holiday, when a Transport Extravaganza is held in a large field adjacent to Havenstreet station.

The remains of a once extensive railway system on the Isle of Wight closed down on 31 December 1966, when the final steam-hauled BR train departed from Ryde Pier Head bound for Shanklin hauled by an 'O2' class. A period of three months followed without any form of BR railway transport on the island during which time engineers were busy installing a third-rail electrification scheme for the remaining 8½ miles of railway on the island – Ryde Pier Head to Shanklin.

Train operations recommenced using former London Transport Underground stock, and later versions of these are still operating today. Perhaps the future of the Isle of Wight railway, known in today's world as the Island Line, is in the balance. Maybe in years to come some closed lines may be reinstated, and maybe even return to steam – but that's only a dream! For trainspotters and steam enthusiasts alike, however, a visit to the Isle of Wight Steam Railway rekindles memories of a country railway run 'how it used to be', and for me and many others the unspoilt countryside and the coastal walks are a magnet that draws us back to the island over and over again.

6

Always on a Sunday

The *Evening News,* Portsmouth's local newspaper in the 1950s and '60s, now the *News,* regularly carried an advertisement from Portsmouth Harbour station for British Railways Sunday Excursion trains departing to various destinations. It was through reading such advertisements that I and my fellow companions whom I had met on Fratton station footbridge first laid our exciting plans to visit engine sheds on Sundays.

These excursions began in early 1957 and were extremely well patronised, continuing successfully for the next five years. However, when they were replaced by the Awayday 'Merrymaker' excursions, an increase in fares and a change of destinations to include venues for children meant that their popularity waned considerably. Departure times from Portsmouth Harbour station were between 9.45 a.m. and 10.35 a.m., depending on the length of the journey. If you were alighting at the excursion's destination your leisure time would usually be about four hours. Sunday excursions were always steam-hauled with at least a nine-carriage train, always including a restaurant or buffet car. On some excursions we would begin with just five or six carriages and on arrival at Eastleigh the train would join up with the corresponding five- or six-carriage excursion originating from Bournemouth or Poole to make up a ten- or twelve-carriage rake.

The empty carriages would have been brought into the Harbour station from Fratton carriage sidings fifteen minutes before departure, usually by one of the three 'C2X' class 0–6–0s allocated to Fratton, numbers 32548, 32549 or 32550. On the excursions departure the 'C2X' would assist as a 'banker' as far as Portsmouth and Southsea (High Level) station, where it would then detach and travel 'light' to Fratton depot ready for its next duty.

The steam locomotives that were rostered for the initial section of these excursions usually to Eastleigh, Basingstoke or Salisbury, depending on the destination, would normally be classes 'T9' 4–4–0s, 'U' 2–6–0s, Standard 4 2–6–0s or Bulleid 4–6–2s in the form of 'West Country' or 'Battle of Britain'. Between 1957 and 1961 I had the pleasure of travelling on no fewer than nineteen of these popular Sunday Excursions – accompanied always by a very enthusiastic bunch of trainspotters, aged between thirteen and twenty-one, and occasionally by our scruffy but knowledgeable middle-aged friend Norman.

It was not uncommon to have a party in excess of ten or twelve travelling on these excursions. Ideally we would occupy two complete compartments, as in those days carriages usually consisted of separate compartments with individual blinds and steam-heating facilities. We also had the option of adding a card table to our compartment, which was always available on request from the train guard. The acquisition of a card table was doubly useful in that we had a base on which to rest our notebooks, Biros, cameras, Ian Allan ABCs and any relevant excursion leaflets, and on the return journey it was used for a game of cards. On many of these excursions, I asked the driver before departure if I could 'cab' the engine and this request was usually granted. The early stages of our journey were sometimes spent playing a game of 'head tennis' with a round balloon being headed into the net luggage racks. There would be two equal sides and to score a goal one had to head the balloon into the opposite side's rack. It was certainly a lot of fun and the first team to reach six was deemed the winner. If nothing else it was rather noisy, but this deterred other passengers from entering our compartment, especially if there were one or two seats remaining!

To avoid being questioned about our age at the Harbour station ticket office when purchasing half-fare excursion tickets we would often obtain a half-fare party ticket for our travelling group from the Co-op Travel Agents, Fratton Road on the Friday or Saturday before our Sunday departure. As some of us looked considerably younger than the others, we found that even at eighteen and nineteen years old we could still get away with half-fares! On the return leg of the excursion, after dark we would fill in our ABCs or Shed Books with our 'cops' of the day. Having completed this and with midnight approaching, some of us would still be active enough to enjoy a game of cards. But often we weary-eyed trainspotters would be jolted awake as the train stopped at a station, and when we eventually saw the Fratton station sign, usually sometime after 1 a.m. on the Monday morning, we knew that our action-packed day of travelling had finally come to an end. I had a 10-minute walk home, usually with Eddie, and needed to be awake by 7 the next morning in order to be at work at Grosvenor Press by 8 a.m.

A few descriptions of incidents from my nineteen Sunday excursions will give an insight into locomotive haulage, routes taken and fares, together with some amusing antics and other incidents which always seemed to happen on these trips.

Cardiff Excursion: Sunday 28 April 1957

We had Fratton-allocated 'U' class 2–6–0 No. 31809 hauling us between Portsmouth Harbour and Salisbury. I travelled with Eddie Rooke, David Copus, Tony Ingram and Terry Hunt, and as with many of these excursions a host of younger trainspotters also travelled; they invariably tagged on to our group when it came to visiting engine sheds! We paid a return fare of 18s 6d to Newport, our destination. Much to our delight we were hauled by a 'Castle' 4–6–0 between Salisbury and Newport (High Street), No. 7035 *Ogmore Castle*. On arrival we lost no time in catching a diesel multiple unit to Griffithstown to visit Pontypool Road depot (86G); here we witnessed a shed crammed full of GWR steam locomotives, seventy-seven in all. Having quickly completed our visit, and with no sign of any shed foreman, we immediately returned to the station and travelled back to Newport.

Our second visit was to Newport (Ebbw Junction) depot (86A), by means of a double-decker bus for Tredegar that took us to the depot entrance. This visit proved to be quite rewarding as we noted no fewer than 126 steam locomotives 'on shed', but before we achieved this we had to avoid the gateman's attention. This we did by cunningly throwing a selection of stones to distract his attention – and while he went out to investigate we crept behind his hut and into the depot! We left via the rear entrance and followed well-trodden pathways across some allotments to get to the dockland area and visit Newport (Pill) depot (86B). Entering this depot without a permit, even on a Sunday, proved to be most difficult. The walled area had a main gate with a gateman staring at you – this was not a case of sneaking round behind as we did at Ebbw Junction! We walked further along the walled area away from the main entrance, where both Eddie and Terry decided to climb the rather high brick wall. They managed this without too many swear words and entered the depot yard and shed, where they noted fifty tank locomotives; Tony, David and I managed to reach the top of the wall, from where we could see the majority of the tank engines. While in the docklands area we could not help but notice the impressive transporter floating bridge, a landmark for many miles.

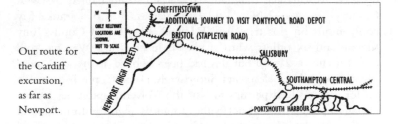

Our route for the Cardiff excursion, as far as Newport.

Having taken our 'Pill', we were faced with an extremely long walk back to Newport (High Street) station. It was early evening, and having experienced almost four hours of non-stop travelling by DMU, bus and on foot, the five of us were much relieved to find a small corner café and sweet shop with an 'Open' sign in the window. Eddie, David and I decided to purchase several enormous 2d ice lollies and continue our walk. Tony and Terry, however, wanted to stop for a small meal, which we objected to on the grounds that since the café was quite crowded we might have to wait some time to be served, and this could make us late in getting back to the station. This disagreement led to a minor fracas between us in the crowded shop and, following the commotion and raised voices, the café proprietor ordered us out – we were distracting his customers. As we were about to leave the café six of the younger trainspotters arrived. They no doubt distracted the café proprietor: we learned later that they had discreetly pocketed numerous packets of sweets! We arrived at the station in plenty of time to catch the return excursion from Cardiff General at 8.40 p.m. It had been a somewhat hectic but enjoyable day, but being trainspotters we had come to expect such punishing schedules. As with many of these Sunday Excursions there was no use of an official permit for engine shed visits; our goal was the thrill and adventure of 'bunking' a shed crammed tight with living steam, and we were determined to succeed. We arrived safely back at Fratton station at 1.30 on the Monday morning – those were the days!

Wolverhampton Excursion: Sunday 2 June 1957

Locomotive haulage between Portsmouth Harbour and Eastleigh was by 'T9' class 4–4–0 No. 30730. At Eastleigh we were joined by the corresponding excursion carriages from Bournemouth, making up a twelve-carriage train, and were then steam-hauled by 'West Country' class 4–6–2 No. 34012 *Launceston* as far as Basingstoke. My companions on this trip were Eddie Rooke, David Copus, Tony Ingram and six others whose names have been lost. We each paid a return fare of 21s 6d but this had been booked at the local travel agents several days beforehand. Surprisingly, David Copus had written off for and received permits to visit the Wolverhampton depots, but having done this we did not bother to go through the formalities of locating the shed foreman to inform him of our arrival (the official procedure). This would have taken up time, and anyway these permits would be filed away in David's cabinet, no doubt to be used again on future visits – with a slight amendment of the date! On this day we visited Oxley depot (84B), where we noted forty-five steam, and then walked to Bushbury depot (38B). This LMS depot was visited very quickly, not that we were in a hurry, but it reeked – we came to the conclusion that a nearby rubbish tip was the cause! Nevertheless we were rewarded with an 'all-steam' depot of thirty-three locomotives including five 'Jubilee' class 4–6–0s. We continued our lengthy walk to Wolverhampton (Stafford Road) depot (84A), where we noted

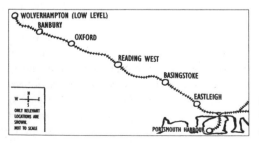

Our route for the Wolverhampton excursion.

seventy-three GWR engines, but we did not attempt to visit the locomotive works situated across the road from the depot.

It had been about a five-mile walk from the station to include all three depot visits, with the sun beating down on our backs, and we were somewhat relieved to return to the Low Level station for a welcome cup of British Railways tea. It was now an appropriate time to tuck into the goodies which we always carried in our haversacks and satchels on these trainspotting trips. My tea was followed by egg sandwiches and a Hales fruit pie – complete bliss after a demanding walk in sweltering conditions!

We caught the 7.30 p.m. return excursion to Portsmouth Harbour, arriving at Fratton station at 1.15 on Monday morning. Another full day of enjoyment had come to an end, but for some of the younger enthusiasts who also travelled on this excursion their day ended even later, being woken up by station staff at Portsmouth Harbour some time after 1.30!

Cardiff Excursion: Sunday 16 June 1957

For some unknown reason no locomotive haulage was recorded on this excursion. Our destination was Bristol, for a return fare of 12s 3d and with a 10.30 a.m. start. I travelled with five other local railway enthusiasts together with five younger trainspotters, all from the Portsmouth area whom we had met on Fratton station footbridge a week or so before the excursion. Having alighted at Bristol (Stapleton Road) station, we faced a considerable amount of walking to visit the three depots in the city. The first visited, or shall we say 'bunked', was the LMS engine shed of Bristol (Barrow Road) depot (22A), where we split up into groups of three to try to look less conspicuous – and it worked. We were thrilled to note two 'Pug' 0–4–0 saddle-tanks Nos 51202 and 51212, together with a further fifty-two steam. Another long walk took us to Bristol (Bath Road) depot (82A). How the eleven of us managed to avoid the shed foreman will forever remain a mystery, as we had to descend a flight of stairs and pass his office to get into the depot – we can only assume that he was having a Sunday afternoon nap! We used the ploy of splitting up into small groups and as a result another depot was successfully 'bunked', where, for the record, we noted fifty-nine steam and two GWR diesel railcars. The impressive arched roof of Temple Meads station was clearly visible from the depot yard.

The final depot to be 'bunked' was reached via the rear entrance of Bath Road depot. This meant a brisk five-minute walk via an official pathway which included crossing a rather desolate double-track railway. Having safely negotiated this we entered Bristol (St Philip's Marsh) depot (82B). This depot produced a grand total of ninety-four steam and thirteen 0–6–0 diesel shunters. Once again we encountered no railway staff and had by now come to the conclusion that being a Sunday, with only minimal movement of locomotives, only a few drivers and firemen were on duty and the foreman was keeping himself to his office.

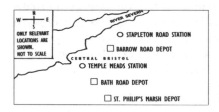

The three locomotive depots 'bunked' in Bristol.

It had been yet another tiring day's trainspotting, with some lengthy walks between depots, but no doubt we would be visiting this area again in the not too distant future as an incredible 207 steam locomotives were written in our notebooks from the three depots visited. After another long walk from St Philip's Marsh, our leg-weary party boarded the return Cardiff Excursion at Stapleton Road at 9.15 p.m. for a well-earned rest before our return to Fratton at 1.30 the next morning.

Cardiff Excursion: Sunday 18 August 1957

This excursion, which included a restaurant car, was steam-hauled between Portsmouth Harbour and Salisbury via Botley, Eastleigh, Chandlers Ford and Romsey by 'West Country' class 4–6–2 locomotive No. 34010 *Sidmouth*; the return fare to Cardiff General was 22s 6d. Two separate groups of enthusiasts travelled on this excursion. I went with Tony Ingram, Vic Coppin, T.F. 'Gaffer' Bleach, John 'Plymouth' Jones and 'Norman'. Eddie Rooke's group consisted of four local enthusiasts, who I believe included Roger 'Domer' Wade, who would visit the small depot of Llantrisant, situated quite a distance north-east of Cardiff. My group was visiting Cardiff (Cathays) with Norman, who needed just one particular 0–6–0 pannier tank to be close to clearing the complete batch of Western Region steam locomotives in existence on BR at this date.

One of our party, whose identity must remain anonymous, had an early morning Sunday paper round to do before catching up with us. The paperboys at his shop all marked up their own papers, and to ensure that we all had plenty to read en route he took care to mark up one extra copy of all the Sunday papers (including *The Sunday Times*) – and brought them all along with him! We somehow found a few quiet moments during the early part of our journey to read these papers, especially the sports section where, during the football season, reports of the previous day's football match involving Portsmouth FC would be our first priority. Reports on the 'other team' twenty miles down the road (Southampton), nicknamed by us 'Pompey' supporters as the 'Scummers', were only given a brief glance, our constant hope being that we would win and they would lose! This 'hate scenario' between the two cities still exists today, with both teams in the Premier League. I remember going to the 'Saints' ground once when Portsmouth were the visitors, and some of our supporters hoisted an enormous banner on the terraces with the words 'PAINE IN THE NECK' clearly visible. Whenever Terry Paine played against us he always proved to be a bit of a handful and, more often than not, scored a goal – hence the somewhat appropriate banner!

When we arrived at Portchester station we had to look out for a new member of our group, a very tall youth we had met previously at Fratton station, nicknamed 'Gaffer' Bleach. As we looked out of the carriage door window he was instantly recognisable by virtue of his too-short jeans and his luminous green socks!

The 'West Country' was taken off at Salisbury and replaced by 'Hall' class 4–6–0 No. 4967 *Shirenewton Hall*. This engine took us through to our destination, Cardiff General, and, as on virtually all these Sunday excursions, the same locomotives were rostered for the corresponding sections of the return journey. This day was particularly full of adventure and excitement for us trainspotters. We successfully 'bunked' five engine sheds, and to say that we covered numerous miles both on foot, by rail and by road would be an understatement, all on a hot summer's day with the sun bearing down on our every move. One particular mode of road transport that we encountered in Cardiff was a 'once in a life-time' experience for us: we travelled between the General station and the docklands area of Cathays on a single-decker trolleybus, a unique design bus that was one of the last of its type in use in Great Britain.

Engine sheds visited on this memorable day were Barry depot (88C), Cardiff (Canton) depot (86C), Cardiff (East Dock) depot (88B), Cardiff (Cathays) depot (88A) and Llantrisant depot (86D). These five visits produced a total of 247 steam, and of note at East Dock were three Rhymney Railway 0–6–2 tanks. Nos 36, 38 and 42. Our separate group visits to depots went as planned and we all met up on Cardiff General station with just enough time to spare for a welcome cup of British Railways tea and a delve into our haversacks for a sandwich or two before boarding the return excursion around 8 p.m. It was noticeable that 'Gaffer' Bleach's luminous green socks had become somewhat 'ordinary' following his visits to dusty, coaldust-infested engine sheds!

Whenever we travelled through the famous Severn Tunnel, hauled by a steam locomotive as on this excursion, the 4½ miles provided us youngsters with an opportunity to have a bit of fun. On entering the tunnel we would open fully the windows of the first corridor carriage behind the locomotive and then retreat to our seats in the centre of the train, leaving the first carriage full of steam and smuts of soot! No doubt passengers made some complaints, but we looked upon our actions as just a spot of fun.

It certainly had been a day to remember, not only for the locomotives noted, the engine sheds 'bunked', the tunnel incident and the trolleybus ride, but also for the sweltering hot weather we had endured while completing our schedule. As with previous Sunday excursions, some of our party had to be brought back from 'the land of nod' by station staff at Portsmouth Harbour station, so demanding had the day been!

Plymouth Excursion: Sunday 20 July 1958

Our party of six departed from Portsmouth Harbour station at 10.30 a.m. on this buffet car excursion. We were steam-hauled via Southampton Central by 'U' class 2–6–0 locomotive No. 31804 to Salisbury, where 'West Country' class 4–6–2 locomotive No. 34035 *Shaftesbury* took over to Plymouth (Friary). We had obtained a 30s half-fare party ticket the previous day from the Co-op Travel

Agents in Fratton Road, and occupied one complete compartment. The now-familiar ritual of 'bunking' engine sheds on these Sunday Excursions was once again undertaken. First we made a visit to the small shed adjacent to Friary station, Plymouth (Friary) depot (83H) – it was a mere formality, noting just sixteen 'on shed'. Our next visit entailed a considerable walk; this was Laira (Plymouth) depot (83D), where we were given a glimpse of future motive power in the form of 'Warship' class main-line diesels, but we did also note eighty steam, including eleven 'Grange' class 4–6–0s.

Having successfully completed our visits to the two Plymouth depots, we walked to North Road station. Our party of six had planned to 'bunk' both Newton Abbot and Exeter depots before boarding the return excursion at Exeter Central station at 8 p.m., but to achieve this we needed to travel on ordinary service trains between Plymouth and Newton Abbot and then on to Exeter (St David's) and to pay the relevant single fares. Being teenagers and willing to take some risks, we decided to split up into groups of two and discreetly hide ourselves in the train toilets! It was lucky for us that no ticket inspector was on the train to Newton Abbot and we managed to get to our destination without being noticed. Our actions were looked upon as great fun but did we ever stop to think of the consequences if we were caught and maybe prosecuted? It would have proved to be rather embarrassing for us, especially if our parents found out.

At Newton Abbot station we noted that we had been steam-hauled by 'Manor' class 4–6–0 No. 7809 *Childrey Manor*. The entrance to the adjoining depot yard was via the unofficial route, direct from the end of the station platform. Newton Abbot depot (83A) had a total of eighty-three GWR steam 'on shed', and we also successfully visited the quite sizeable depot works. Returning to the station, we then travelled to Exeter by diesel multiple unit; I only remember this section of our journey vaguely, but we probably used our return excursion tickets and hoped that no ticket inspectors would appear!

Exeter depot (83C) was next to be visited. Once again it was not only 'bunked' but our party scampered directly from the train door at St David's station and into the engine shed yard, where there were no railwaymen nearby to see us – definitely an illegal entry! At this depot we noted twenty-seven Western Region steam and one solitary LMS '8F' class 2–8–0. On leaving the depot we walked through the streets of Exeter and were relieved to find a chip shop. Needless to say, we devoured sixpenny bags of chips as we walked towards Central station, washing them down with swigs of the Tizer or lemonade we had brought in our haversacks. After quite an eventful day, with many miles of walking needed to make the planned engine shed visits, we arrived at Exeter Central station looking forward to a comfortable rest on the journey home. As usual, we underlined our 'cops' and in the later stage of our journey played a lengthy game of cards before being overcome by sleep. We arrived back at Fratton at 1.15 on Monday morning, a very tired group of trainspotters.

We travelled on many Sunday excursions during 1957 and 1958, all filled with the same spirit of adventure, and all including 'bunking' of locomotive depots and the amusing incidents that always seemed to happen to us. I would like to have described them all but will finish this chapter with some brief accounts.

We visited Nottingham in both 1957 and 1958, with Colwick (38A), Nottingham (16A) and Toton (18A) depots all successfully 'bunked'; on the 1958 excursion we were steam-hauled between Banbury and Nottingham (Victoria) via Woodford Halse, Rugby and Leicester by Eastern Region 'B1' class 4–6–0 No. 61271.

We went to Cheltenham in December 1957, with Cheltenham depot visited and a double-decker bus ride to visit the two Gloucester depots of Horton Road (85B) and Barnwood (22A) – the latter being an LMS depot. Most interestingly on that day were the four changes of locomotive haulage that took place – 'U' class 2–6–0 No. 31808 from Portsmouth to Eastleigh, 'West Country' class 4–6–2 No. 34040 *Crewkerne* to Salisbury, 'County' class 4–6–0 No. 1028 *County of Warwick* to Bristol (Temple Meads) and Class 5 4–6–0 No. 44919 to Cheltenham, banked out of Bristol by '4F' class 0–6–0 No. 43926. I believe this was the first of many trainspotting trips in the company of Dave Bodenham.

We went to Weymouth on 25 May 1958, on a ten-carriage buffet car excursion steam-hauled throughout by Fratton-allocated 'U' class 2–6–0 No. 31637 via Southampton Central, Brockenhurst and Bournemouth. Sheds 'bunked' were Weymouth (71G), Bournemouth (71B) and Eastleigh (71A), the latter being reached illegally via Southampton Central and Swaythling – we should have paid a single fare! We returned to Portsmouth via Botley and Fareham steam-hauled by Standard class 4 4–6–0 No. 75079.

7

Ten Go into the Unknown

Portsmouth in the late 1950s had many thriving groups of trainspotters, most of whom gathered at some time or other on Fratton station footbridge, but there were many more groups such as those attached to youth clubs and schools whose leaders encouraged teenagers to participate in what they thought was a comparatively harmless and safe hobby involving group railtrips to various areas of Great Britain. Eddie Rooke and David Copus attended Portsmouth Southern Grammar School for Boys, which possessed quite an active 00-gauge model railway club of which David was a founder member; before too long this club became an even more active trainspotting club! Although I attended a different school, I still had the pleasure of joining them on several of their trips, as did others, including Terry Hunt, who attended Southsea Modern School.

One particular three-day trainspotting trip originated with the school club, and to say that it was extraordinary would be an understatement. It was truly an 'adventure into the unknown'. Regrettably I could not be a part of this trip because of other commitments but it does give an indication of the incidents and, at times, dangers that teenagers experienced in order to widen their knowledge of the British Railways system. They learned to locate railway installations with precision by taking with them a small booklet, *The British Railways Locomotive Shed Directory*, they gained much geographical knowledge, and of course they also began to recognise the numerous BR steam locomotive classes that existed in those days. Above all, they enjoyed the freedom and spirit of adventure which every trainspotting trip brought. An application for engine shed permits should have been a priority on any such trip, but official permits were only used infrequently, and when they were obtained no one bothered to produce them at depots unless they were asked for! This trip was one of those undertaken without permits.

Ten teenagers from the Portsmouth area, including Terry Hunt, Charlie Best and 'Gaffer' Bleach, were led by the two most senior railway enthusiasts, Eddie Rooke and David Copus, on an engine shed tour of the West Midlands between 1 and 3 January 1958. New Year's Day was not a public holiday in those days and trains were running a normal service. The group had made no sleeping arrangements for their two nights away, and in fact some of the thirteen- to fifteen-year-olds had never been away from home overnight before. Little did they realise at the start of their adventure what would happen later.

Wednesday 1 January was the first day of their mammoth three-day railway journey. They left Fratton at 6 a.m. to travel via Eastleigh and Basingstoke to Reading (General). Here they changed trains and travelled to Swindon to visit the locomotive works, where there were three brand-new steam locomotives under construction: '9F' class 2–10–0 Nos 92184, 92185 and 92186. They moved on to 'bunk' depots at Worcester (85A) and then Kidderminster (85D) before ending the day at Wolverhampton (Low Level) railway station, where Eddie and David planned to spend the night in the waiting-room. All went to plan until just before midnight when the local police paid them a visit and pointed out that they had to move on. When the police asked why ten teenagers were out at this time of night, the story was told that they were on a three-day trainspotting trip of the area. I think the police felt sorry for them, especially the younger boys, intending to spend the night in the station waiting-room in temperatures that were anything but normal. The police insisted that the ten youths go with an officer to the local police station, where an attempt would be made to find them a hostel or safe accommodation for the night.

Much to my friends' amazement, the transport from the railway station to the police station came in the form of a 'Black Maria'. Once at the police station, however, it became apparent following some brief telephone calls that no overnight accommodation was available. The Wolverhampton police must be commended on their next actions: they provided the youths with cells containing bunk beds, fed them with jam doughnuts and cups of hot drinking chocolate and even gave them an early morning call at 6 a.m. so that they could continue their trainspotting visits! Having thanked the police for their generous hospitality, the group, now fully refreshed, moved into the city in what could only be described as freezing conditions.

It was now Thursday 2 January, and they made early morning visits to all three locomotive depots in Wolverhampton and, additionally, Stafford Road Works, all duly 'bunked' before 8.45 a.m. The order of visits was Wolverhampton (Stafford Road), Oxley (84B) and Bushbury (3B), and it is surprising that ten youths illegally wandering around these depots in icy and slippery conditions were not spotted by the foremen. No doubt Eddie and David used their expertise and split them into small groups. This method had been tried and proved in previous engine shed visits and it goes without saying that this procedure was repeated throughout that day and the next. All their travel between depots was by rail, and the next in line for 'bunking' were Walsall (3C), Bescot (3A), Stourbridge Junction (84F), Tyseley (84E) and finally, towards the end of the day as they moved into the city of Birmingham, Monument Lane (3E). The motley crew must have looked like ragamuffins as they pursued their tight timetable; luckily they survived the icy conditions. A chip shop visit proved to be pure bliss! It must have been an exceptionally hectic day's travelling, covering many miles, on top of which they had to contend with freezing conditions, not to mention a heavy fall of snow! Some of the more interesting notings from this day were at Oxley depot, where they were quite surprised to see diminutive '0F' class (Pug) 0–4–0 saddle-tank No. 51204 of 1891 vintage, and at Monument Lane depot, where a brace of Compounds were noted – 4–4–0s Nos 40936 and 41090.

I doubt whether the West Midlands police would have taken pity on a group of ten youths if they found them for a second night running at a main-line railway station, namely Birmingham (New Street), but the leaders had a plan. That evening the group went to the cinema and saw *The Pride and the Passion*, starring Cary Grant and Sophia Loren. Following this well-earned rest – during which some fell asleep – they walked the streets of central Birmingham for at least two hours, visiting a fish and chip shop to help combat the freezing temperatures. They had worked on the theory that the police visited the main-line stations shortly after the public houses had called last orders so that they could move on the drunks and the inevitable tramp or two. This turned out to be correct, as the group arrived at New Street station well after midnight and were rewarded with an uninterrupted night in the relative comfort of the hard wooden seats of the station waiting room.

Thursday 3 January, their third day in the West Midlands, began early. The station clock told them it was exactly 5.25 a.m. as they made their way from New Street station around Birmingham to their first depot 'bunking' of the day at Saltley (21A). A succession of depots followed, including Aston (3D), and while heading back towards Portsmouth they took in Leamington Spa (84D), Banbury (84C), Oxford (81F), Didcot (81E) and finally Reading (81D).

The travel-weary teenagers had experienced a most extraordinary trainspotting adventure. As they travelled home between Reading and Portsmouth they had time to reflect on their three-day trip and probably asked themselves the question, 'Would we do it again at some other location and date?' I think their answer would be 'Yes', as teenagers of that era were always looking for adventure and the harmless hobby of trainspotting gave them just that.

Eddie Rooke had by now gained a keen interest in developing and printing his own photographs. His experimenting unfortunately produced some very mixed results and he did not pursue the interest further. He took a handful of photographs on this trip which he developed and printed himself and with all due respect the three reproduced for this chapter, despite the lost locations of two, appear to be remarkably clear compared with the others.

8

No Time to Stop

Whether our trainspotting trips took up a day, a weekend or even a full week, to stop for food and drink at a café or restaurant was virtually unknown. On the rare occasions that it happened it seemed quite a luxury. As you have probably guessed, we rarely thought about the need for food when planning. In fact these trips always turned out to be a kind of self-imposed torture, but what kept us motivated was the magic and fascination of knowing that the next engine shed visit would produce more living steam locomotives and this spurred us on to complete our demanding timetable, forsaking any stops for food. But it would be wrong to say that we neither ate nor drank. We all carried some type of satchel or haversack containing a selection of food and drink on each trip, although there were no set times or locations for consuming these goodies.

The haversack I took on nearly every trip had a history attached to it. It began its life as my mum's potato sack but when it was replaced with an up-to-date plastic container I persuaded mum to cut it up and sew the pieces together on her treadle-operated Singer sewing machine. My plea was answered and a haversack was born! What delights this haversack used to contain on our railway trips: smelly egg sandwiches, a bottle of diluted orange squash or Tizer, and my favourite, a Hales individually boxed apricot fruit pie, for the sum of just 1s 7d in the late 1950s! And invariably there was the standard packet of Smith's crisps with the salt contained in a separate twist of blue paper.

Not only did my haversack contain food and drink but there were also various items of attire. One was a genuine Charlotte Street cloth cap (this street was famous in the centre of Portsmouth for its open market). These caps would be donned whenever the heavens opened and we would wear them with some dignity. Also important was the plastic mac or 'Pak-a-Mac'. In my days this was the forerunner of the anorak. In today's world the anorak promotes a somewhat false image of a trainspotter and it annoys me to be put in this category when I never wore an anorak – they did not become popular until the end of the 1960s. On this subject, why do the media always associate items such as a pair of wire-rimmed glasses with the image of a trainspotter?

Not carried in the haversack but an essential part of every trainspotting trip was my pair of brown 'Tuf' lace-up shoes. These were worn between the mid-1950s and 1968 and certainly lived up to their name: they came into contact with oil, coal dust, grease, mud, rain, ice and snow and they never needed their soles replacing! These shoes are still in my proud possession today.

Apart from the obvious notebooks, Biros and sometimes a camera, we would occasionally take an official motive power depot permit with us, but if David Copus was included in our party we would carry a suitably amended wad of previously used permits relating to our visits of the day. If an occasion arose where we were stopped by the shed foreman asking for our permit, the date on David's permit was sure to have become illegible because of some smart smudging of the ink!

Also in the haversack would be our Ian Allan ABC combined volume of *British Railways Locomotives*, the *Loco Shed Book* and *The British Locomotive Shed Directory*. These were taken on most trips and we would proudly underline the day's 'cops' in the two former books on the return journey – this was the only part of the day when we had some time on our hands.

9

Kings Cross via Doncaster

A very memorable trainspotting trip by both rail and road took place between Saturday 30 August and Monday 1 September 1958. My travelling companions for this long weekend were Jim 'Jimpy' Lawrence, Charlie Best, Jack Knowler and David Greenfield, all from Portsmouth, but the coach trip to Doncaster actually started from London and was organised by a Mr Ernie Middleton of the North London Locospotters Club. As we could not guarantee arriving at the coach departure point at York Way, adjacent to Kings Cross station, by 8 a.m. on the Sunday, we decided to travel to London (Victoria) by train, purchasing single tickets on the Saturday afternoon.

We were able to visit several main-line terminus stations, including St Pancras, Euston and Liverpool Street, before ending up at Kings Cross station late that evening. Some interesting scenes were recorded at these stations, such as 'Britannia' class 4–6–2 No. 70044 *Earl Haig* at Euston letting off steam at the arrival end of the station, while, in complete contrast, at the far end of one of the departure platforms diesel-electric locomotive No. 10001 was quietly awaiting its departure on a passenger train for Scotland. Our visit to Liverpool Street station coincided with the rush hour and consequently we noted no fewer than thirty-eight steam and four main-line diesels in a fifty-five-minute visit! It seemed that 'Britannia' class locomotives were in charge of many of the steam-hauled passenger trains: some of those noted were Nos 70000 *Britannia*, 70003 *John Bunyan*, 70005 *John Milton*, 70008 *Black Prince*, 70010 *Owen Glendower*, 70011 *Hotspur* and 70039 *Sir Christopher Wren*.

My haversack was as usual well stocked with food and drink, and later that evening I eagerly consumed cheese and pickle sandwiches and swigged orange squash while sitting on some porters' wooden trucks at the far end of Kings Cross station's longest platform. Meanwhile, there were constant arrivals and departures of passenger trains, either side of our platform – no doubt our sandwiches contained some soot!

As it was quite a warm summer's evening, we decided to use as beds the porters' wooden trolleys on which we had eaten our supper. We used our satchels and haversacks to cushion our heads and our checked cloth caps and our trusty plastic macs proved sufficient to keep out any night-time chills. This was our bed and breakfast accommodation, courtesy of British Railways – unbelievably no railway staff approached us during the night. Two of our friends, Jack Knowler and David Greenfield, being rather refined, decided against this 'roughing it' – they telephoned some nearby relatives and arranged some overnight accommodation. Before they left we arranged to meet them at 8 a.m. the next day in York Way.

Amid the hissing, clanking and general movements of a steady flow of steam locomotives throughout the night, sleep was almost impossible for Jim and me but Charlie Best, with only a plastic mac covering him, was asleep in no time and his loud incessant snoring kept us both amused! While Charlie slept we made several trips to nearby St Pancras station, on one of which we were rewarded with the sight of 'Jubilee' class 4–6–0 No. 45569 *Tasmania*.

We spent several hours away from Kings Cross station, and apart from visiting St Pancras station we also visited a fish and chip shop where we had our supper. Returning to the station platform and the porters' trolleys, we found that Charlie was still fast asleep. It must have been around 4.30 a.m. that the whistle of a steam engine awoke Charlie, at which he immediately stood up, draped in his plastic mac and cloth cap – I recall his words exactly: 'Where am I?' My breakfast that morning consisted of the remainder of the previous day's sandwiches, now somewhat flattened by using the haversack as a pillow and also rather stale, washed down with yet more Tizer direct from the bottle, and followed by a bag of Smith's crisps. As we left the station, we were glad to see some vending machines and topped up our resources for the coming day with cartons of milk and bars of chocolate.

We were now fully refreshed as we made our way in the bright early morning sunshine to Kings Cross depot (34A) via York Way, entering the yard at exactly 5.40 a.m. – it goes without saying that we did not have a permit for this visit. It was a magnificent sight to see the shed and yards crammed full of steam locomotives, of which we noted ninety-five; the sight of ten Gresley 'A4' class streamlined Pacifics was a trainspotter's dream, and one of these was that famous engine No. 60022 *Mallard*, which in 1938 attained a world speed record for steam of 126 mph. We negotiated the depot without being noticed and walked back to the station. Following a quick wash and brush up we walked to York Way, where at around 8 a.m. we once again met up with Jack Knowler and David Greenfield.

We were introduced to Ernie Middleton, the coach trip organiser, and then we settled down in the luxury of a coach seat for an 8.15 a.m. start. The party consisted of thirty-five railway enthusiasts. Both Jim and I dozed off as soon as we sat down, of course, and my next recollection is being awoken by the jolt of the coach stopping at the entrance to Grantham depot (35B). What happened next will always be etched in my memory. On entering the depot yard our thirty-five-strong party was surprisingly, it being early on a Sunday morning, met by the shed foreman. He promptly demanded in a loud voice 'Who's in charge?' 'I am,' replied Ernie. The foreman demanded to see our permit of visit. 'I don't have a permit', Ernie replied. The foreman looked on in amazement as we proceeded with our visit to Grantham depot. As Ernie said to us, 'There are thirty-five of us, but only one foreman.' He urged us not to hang about but to get back to the waiting coach as soon as possible. Meanwhile, the foreman retreated to his office, obviously out-numbered! This depot saw forty-three steam 'on shed' which included just nine main-line Pacifics.

Our next engine shed visit (actually, Ernie did have permits for most depots, and obviously for Doncaster Works) was the small three-lane Tuxford (40D) where we saw only fourteen Eastern Region steam 'on shed'. After leaving this location the coach soon made a welcome stop at a transport café, where I recall eagerly tucking into baked beans on toast and several cups of piping hot tea, followed by chocolate biscuits. The coach continued to the two small Retford depots, only 700 yards apart, of the Great Central and the Great Eastern, both sharing the same code of 36E. I cabbed a unique '1P' class 0–4–4 tank engine of 1889 vintage and a Great Northern depot, No. 58065. Getting nearer our destination, we next visited Ranskill Wagon Works where we noted two 0–4–0 steam locomotives, Nos 3 and 4.

At Doncaster depot (36A) we recorded a total of 120 steam 'on shed' and five diesel shunters; one locomotive of special note was 'W1' class 4–6–4 streamlined type No. 60700, reputed to be the most powerful main-line steam locomotive in Great Britain. The icing on the cake was our official visit with a guide to Doncaster Works, noting eighty-seven steam, all in various stages of repair. This works was famous for its construction of many BR steam locomotives, including No. 60022 *Mallard* and No. 60103 *Flying Scotsman*, but on this visit, as a sign of the changing times, we noted under construction three main-line electric locomotives intended for the Southern Region, Nos E5000, E5001 and E5002.

We travelled next to Mexborough depot (36B). Here we were greeted with a depot filled to its limit with predominantly freight steam classes, including twenty-three WD 2–8–0s. This was one of the depots that Ernie had no permit to visit, but having scattered ourselves into small groups we somehow managed to evade the foreman. Continuing south, we then made a visit to a depot with no steam locomotives, Wath, a sub-depot of Mexborough. Moving on, we visited the Rotherham area depot of Canklow (19C), where steam was once again dominant. Two small 0–6–0 '1F' class tank engines, Nos 41835 and 41875, of a class introduced in 1878, were noted, their odd-looking appearance being highlighted by their cut-back cabs.

Finally, the coach took us to our last engine shed visit, Newark, a sub-depot of Retford, where I have memories of cabbing '1P' class 0–4–0 tank No. 58085. Now that our visits were finished, it should have been a fairly quick run back to York Way in London, transfer by underground train to Waterloo and arrival home in Portsmouth late on the Sunday evening. Things do not always go as planned, however: on our journey south we were caught up in a huge traffic jam and consequently arrived back in London far too late to connect with the last train from Waterloo to Portsmouth. There was only one solution – we would return to the porters' wooden trolleys on Kings Cross station for a second night running!

The same procedure as the previous night took place, Jack and David retreating to their relatives' house nearby, while Jim, Charlie and I settled down on the trolleys wearing our plastic macs and cloth caps as protection against the weather. We need not have bothered, as it was a very warm night. Supper was several bars of chocolate and a cup of tea from the station vending machines. Locomotive movements appeared less intense than the previous night, perhaps because it was a Sunday or maybe we were tired. Anyway, we dozed off quickly. When I next checked my watch it was 5.35 a.m.: I gave Jim a nudge and he soon awoke. We now indulged in some trainspotting, as a selection of steam locomotives had appeared while we were sleeping; from my notes we saw Pacifics Nos 60044 *Melton*, 60136 *Alcazar* and 60142 *Edward Fletcher*.

After leaving our overnight sleeping accommodation we had the bliss of a most welcome wash and brush-up in the gents at Kings Cross, and having been reunited with Jack and David we were in a fairly happy mood. This was soon dampened when we realised that after buying single tickets on the forward journey on Saturday, some of us did not have sufficient funds to get us home to Portsmouth.

Following a brief discussion, some of our party, who shall remain anonymous, decided to make their way home to Fratton via the 'Charlie Best route'. This method of 'bunking' using specific non-corridor trains was essential to avoid being seen by a ticket collector or inspector. The route was anything but direct! They travelled apparently from somewhere on the tube train, eventually arriving at New Cross Gate, then to Norwood, Horsham, Littlehampton and Barnham to Fratton. The group arrived home safely about two hours after the rest of us, very tired, but at the same time much relieved that 'Charlie's route' had worked for them.

At last I was able to make my way home from Fratton station to what must have been some rather anxious parents awaiting my return. I quickly deposited my Tuf shoes and my haversack in the hallway and feeling exhausted immediately retired to my bedroom. My mother brought me a cup of tea and some beans on toast – I drank the tea and sleep overcame me. Four hours later I awoke to find baked beans scattered all over the bed!

Mentioning this cunning, well-planned route of 'bunking' by train between London and Portsmouth brings to mind other methods also meticulously planned in the late 1950s by teenage trainspotters.

I remember that you could go a long way by purchasing a one penny platform ticket. In those days the widespread use of non-corridor coaching stock by British Railways was fairly common, thereby protecting you from ticket inspectors. To get from Portsmouth to London, the easiest method was either to purchase a platform ticket or, to be safer, purchase a return ticket between Fratton and Havant (a distance of about 6 miles), then, on arrival at Guildford, alight and cross the footbridge, and catch the non-corridor electric unit train to Victoria, travelling via Effingham Junction. When this particular train reached Victoria it always entered the platform adjoining the wide taxi rank road and it was quite easy to walk down the centre of this, thereby avoiding the ticket collector!

There were many similar schemes employed by certain of my friends, mainly centred around the use of platform tickets or buying short-distance local return tickets to get you off the train at our home station. Quite often, knowledge of certain stations gained from previous trainspotting trips and reading the trainspotter's bible, *The British Locomotive Shed Directory*, enabled them to alight from the train without seeing ticket collectors. The most common way to leave the station would be to walk off the end of your arrival platform directly into the engine shed yard or building. This method was successful at many stations, including Oxford, Bournemouth,

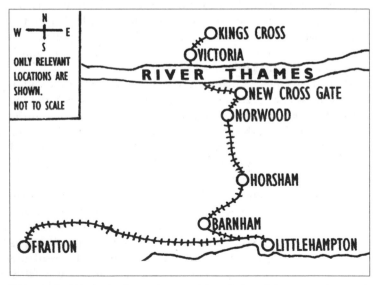

This was the 'Charlie Best' route between Kings Cross and Fratton, via Norwood, Horsham and Littlehampton, using specific non-corridor trains.

Severn Tunnel Junction, Newton Abbot, Exeter (St David's) and Salisbury. The last mentioned was a somewhat lengthy walk, exposed to passing trains! Reading General was one station, along with several others, where upon arrival at a specific platform, you could avoid the ticket collector by going out through the parcels office.

One of the classic trips that I was told about happened on one of the popular Sunday excursion trains from Portsmouth Harbour station to Cardiff General in the late 1950s. Twelve of my trainspotting friends travelled, but only *one* purchased an official ticket to travel! The others used platform tickets to get on the train at Portsmouth Harbour, and relied upon the one legitimate traveller to buy them platform tickets to get them off the train on their arrival at Cardiff (in those days there were never any ticket collectors on the Sunday excursions, even though they were corridor trains).

On the return journey, on reaching Fratton, they had to make sure that they were in the fourth carriage from the front, as this carriage always stopped directly opposite the gentlemen's toilet, where they hid until the ticket collector had returned to his quarters, pending the arrival of the next train! Anyway, when the excursion arrived at 1.30 a.m. on the Monday morning, the chance of a ticket collector being on duty was negligible. Such cunning plans involving preying on non-corridor trains and avoiding the ticket collector must have involved considerable planning, and they always seemed to be successful it would be out of the question to even think about such plans when travelling on today's railways in Britain! You could say that back then my friends certainly had a 'Cheap Day Return!'

10

Look in the Directory

I look upon teenagers in today's world as a completely different breed compared with those from the era in which I grew up. Of course, with the introduction of videos and computers, things I never had, today's youth have so many avenues open to explore, to gain knowledge and enjoyment from. I don't despise this, as any new technology not only improves one's lifestyle but more importantly promotes employment.

When I left Kingston Modern School for Boys in December 1956, television had not yet reached the classroom, and it was not until the early 1960s that my parents could afford such a luxury, albeit a Bakelite set with just the solitary BBC1 channel. Television was a new toy for us lads, and in the late 1950s when Charlie Best's parents bought a set the living-room of their small terraced house in the Somers Road area of Portsmouth attracted an audience of his mates, all marvelling at such new heights of technology. But his parents were not so amused as countless cups of tea had to be made for us, and the biscuit tin was often left bare!

Charlie was a very big Elvis Presley fan, and whenever we visited Charlie's house we were always treated to the sound of Elvis's early 33rpm albums. When the record-player was off we would listen to Radio Luxembourg on Radio Relay which Charlie's parents had installed. We would often play cards (for quite considerable sums) until the early hours of the morning. Charlie's mother, Lil, would often play too, a woman you would not wish to upset. She looked like a large version of Nora Batty, minus the stockings but with a permanent fag in her mouth! In contrast Bill, Charlie's stepfather, was small, henpecked and resembled Barney Rubble from *The Flintstones*. Nevertheless, we were always made very welcome there, despite them having to refill the teapot at frequent intervals!

The 1950s and the 1960s were halcyon days, when teenagers went about their hobbies quietly and discreetly, and my interest of trainspotting just happened to be one of those pastimes. The parents of many of my friends were also a part of our lives and we would often meet whenever I visited my friends' homes. Like my own mother and father, they lived in an era when discipline was paramount and their sons and daughters appreciated any words of encouragement given. We would certainly inform them whenever we took a long weekend or maybe a week-long railway trip that involved being away from home, but we never told them that our bed and breakfast accommodation would be a station waiting-room, platform or maybe an overnight train. If we had I don't think too many of our trips would have even started! I do not recall ever contacting my parents during one of my lengthy railway trips and the same applied to my friends; we never had the inclination to telephone or even send a postcard, and our waiting parents must have felt quite relieved to see us return home safely.

We were a bunch of teenagers who were always looking for adventure, not only on our trainspotting trips but also when out walking the streets of our city. Girls were never far from our thoughts and our youth club connection meant a constant supply, whom we would often arrange to meet at coffee bars and in the shopping area of Commercial Road. At no time did we cause any serious damage to property or other people, we never committed any violence and we never became involved with drugs. Also, that disgraceful disfigurement known today as graffiti was unheard of. That's not to say we were all good boys, however. We were never known as a gang and we did not vandalise trains ourselves, but I often travelled with others who took the liberty to throw card tables out of the train window on Fareham viaduct and hurl lumps of Welsh coal at greenhouses as we passed Romsey late at night. Looking back on actions like this it is difficult to believe that the people involved escaped being caught in the act and that their foolishness caused no injuries to the general public. If we had done something very wrong and it became known to our parents, this would often culminate in a severe telling off or, in my case, a few sharp whacks across the backside from my dad's leather belt – a timely reminder that caused some discomfort. This medicine was hard to take, but looking back I realise that he was strict but fair. Unfortunately, in today's world such actions are looked upon as inflicting cruelty and are illegal. One wonders whether we would see less violence and fewer muggings on the streets if those strict but fair parental days ever returned. Anyway, that's another story.

David Copus was usually at the forefront of many an idea in which we would all eventually get involved. One such scheme always brings a wry smile and a few memories flooding back. David's idea was to scan the pages of the local telephone directory and pick out unusual names. Quite a few of these oddly named people would at some time or other have received a telephone call from a giggling group of teenagers crammed tight in a local call box! A Mr Belcher came in for quite a bashing, as did a Mr Crudass, a Mr Iggo and a Mr Crockett. The last mentioned happened to be my local hairdresser in St Mary's Road and whenever I entered his establishment for a dome scrape (haircut) I needed to keep my conversation to a minimum for obvious reasons! The two lines of the following song, to that famous tune of 'Davy Crockett', are what we used to sing to him from a telephone box:

Davy, Davy Crockett,
King of the dome scrapers.

Another two directory names that were preyed upon were a Mr Parrott and a Mr Funnell. These two would be treated to renditions of 'Land of Hope and Glory', changed to 'Land of Parrott and Funnell'. A group of about five youths would pack into a telephone booth and try to sing the full four verses which David had composed. It always turned out to be a bit of a struggle, as by the end of the first verse we would either be in fits of laughter or our money would have run out! The first two verses went something like this:

Land of Parrott and Funnell,
Runker on the throne.
Wiggins in the constabulary,
Trying to scrape his dome.

Here comes V.D. Raper,
From the crunnery.
He's with Billy Belcher,
Drinking synthetic tea.

With a list of names as long as your arm all picked from the local directory you would have thought that would all have ended there, but no, numerous additional silly words were introduced such as Garst, Gunge, Gizzard, Spon, Sloother, Croother, Yonge and Noddy. I recall visiting Fratton engine shed one Saturday morning in the company of David and several other enthusiasts all with pocketfuls of white chalk. That morning numerous engines received silly names chalked boldly on their side tanks or tenders and the local railwaymen probably realised that those damn trainspotters had been visiting again! Unbelievably, some of the locomotives adorned with these names were sent out on their duties. Later that day we were quite surprised to see a 'U' class 2–6–0 passing through Fratton station with a passenger train for Salisbury with the words 'Flying Gizzard' chalked in large capital letters on its tender; we also saw 'E4' class 0–6–2 tank No. 32495 on shunting duties with 'Noddy' displayed on the side tank!

We were growing up in the early years of rock and roll and skiffle, and one of our most popular artists was Lonnie Donegan, who produced such skiffle classics as 'Rock Island Line' (appropriately a railway theme) and 'Battle of New Orleans'. The latter song inspired David and his mates to put their own words to its tune, incorporating another of our telephone directory names – Belcher. I can't remember us ever completing the full three verses over the telephone to the gentleman – by the end of the first verse we would be reduced to a giggling mass and would have to replace the receiver. We never did find out his first name but we christened him 'Billy'. The words went like this:

In 1840, we took a little run,
Down to Belcher's Crunnery along with Henry Crun;
We took some rice and some synthetic tea;
And we met up with the oozing garsts at Belcher's Crunnery.

Well, we released a belch, but the garsts kept a comin';
But they had less cream doughnuts than they had a while ago;
We belched once more and they began an oozing;
Out of Albert's Oghouse where the gizzard goats do grow.

continued overleaf

Crun said we would take 'em by surprise;
If we fired our tea urns straight into their eyes;
Then all of a sudden there was a great big foam;
And out walked Belcher with a tea urn on his dome.

These silly songs became quite well known and were even sung on some of our railway trips; some of the younger trainspotters who accompanied us on engine shed visits were also being converted, including Doug Willis, Mike Chapman, Mike Dooley, Roy Wiltshire, Dave Woolley, Michael Ashcroft and Vic Coppin. The list of silly names, some real and some fictitious, started off as an 8 × 10in piece of paper, but it circulated for nearly two years, during which it was either handed on or posted to all our pals, all of whom added their own contribution just like a 'chain letter', and that sheet of paper ended up almost three feet long, tightly crammed with names. This became known as the 'Crudhopper Letter' and remained in David's possession for many years.

Looking back and reflecting on our total inanity, I wonder how we gained so much satisfaction and enjoyment from a list of names originally taken at random from the local telephone directory, 99 per cent of whom we never knew or even met! Utter madness!

11

Footbridge of Delight

Why did we spend nearly all day trainspotting from Fratton station footbridge? Quite simply, because of the attraction of the trains; steam and electric units always held a special fascination, and there were other forms of transport, and also local characters.

One notable individual, a middle-aged trainspotter called Norman, whose hallmarks were a fag hanging from his mouth and a greasy jacket that had seen better days. He boasted that he only needed ten GWR steam to clear the Region. Despite his scruffy appearance we were the best of friends and he accompanied us on several Sunday excursions.

Another much-respected character, marvelled at not only by us railway enthusiasts but also by the general public, was the resident policeman on point duty on Fratton Bridge. He stood on a wooden plinth in the centre of the road and controlled traffic from the six roads converging. At times of peak traffic we would wander from the footbridge along Goldsmith Avenue so we could note both the railway movements and those of PC Alec 'Dutchie' Holland. At the height of the evening rushhour his arms would be constantly waving drivers to stop, start or turn left or right, his actions being in fact equivalent to several sets of traffic lights!

This popular policeman, nicknamed 'PC Wonderful', carried out these duties for many years, and when the festive season arrived drivers would show their appreciation of his efforts by briefly pausing at his wooden plinth and placing a present at his feet! Sadly, he is no longer with us, and genuine characters of his type do not seem to exist today. His duties have now been replaced by three sets of traffic lights.

Up to the summer of 1963 Goldsmith Avenue and Fratton Bridge were the route for a friendly, pollution-free mode of transport – the trolleybus. Sometimes a trolleybus driver would take the turn too fast into Goldsmith Avenue and the bus poles would come off the wires on Fratton Bridge. We trainspotters often witnessed this; if it happened during the rushhour poor old 'Dutchie' Holland gained an extra job – to signal the traffic around the stricken trolley-bus until the driver re-poled. This only took a matter of minutes and then the bus would be on its way.

Once or twice each year a special train would arrive on Platform 3 at Fratton station: this train transported live animals belonging to Bertram Mills' Circus. I noted 'N' class 2–6–0 No. 31824 employed on such a train on Sunday 9 October 1960. Following its arrival at the station the train travelled slowly past Fratton West signal-box and then reversed into the Fyffes Banana siding adjacent to Goldsmith Avenue. Here we could see many elephants being off-loaded and led by hand through the streets to Southsea Common, where the circus was set up in large marquees. Obviously, this particular siding was more often witness to the occasional banana train depositing its load to be distributed to the markets and shops of Portsmouth. Such banana trains would pick up their load from Southampton Docks and travel via St Denys and Netley to Fratton. Although a wide variety of steam locomotive classes would be used for this duty, it was in the main Standard class 4 2–6–0s, 'U' class 2–6–0s, Ivatt tanks and 'Q1' class 0–6–0s that were noted.

We would often pick up David Copus from his house, which was almost opposite the entrance to Fratton locomotive depot (70F), when we went to visit the depot. This visit would often follow a dinner break from our trainspotting on the station footbridge, when locomotives that we had missed during our absence would have been 'on shed'. First we had to avoid the 'Old B' as he was known, Mr Butler, the engine shed foreman. He always seemed to see us before we saw him and as a result we were ejected more times than I care to remember. Even so, we kept visiting the depot and learnt that entering the yard via the side of the old pump house building was the best way to avoid him. It is ironic that our own locomotive depot proved to be the most difficult to 'bunk', yet we safely negotiated numerous other depots all over Great Britain without an official permit. Perhaps it was because the 'Old B' recognised us, since we had made so many unsuccessful visits!

One source of amusement for us railway enthusiasts gathered on the footbridge was to see an electric unit train with one of its windows fully opened proceed through the carriage washing unit – some of the seats must have had a severe drenching! This unit did have its advantages especially when a steam locomotive reversed its carriages through the wash on a hot summer's day; the engine crew would deliberately take the tender full of coal through the water jets, to dampen the coal and keep the risk of dust blowing into the cab to a minimum.

Football excursions and specials were nearly all steam-hauled in and out of Portsmouth, certainly up to the mid-1960s. Whenever a football special brought visiting supporters into Portsmouth for a match at Fratton Park, it would terminate at Fratton station, Platform 3. The scurrying hordes of supporters would then cross the footbridge into Goldsmith Avenue and make the ten-minute

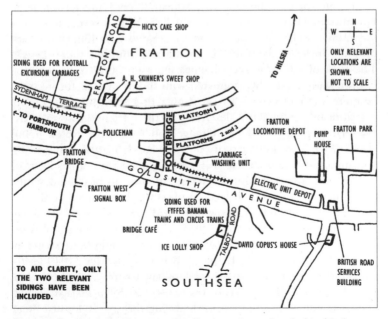

These are the relevant locations centred on Fratton station, as described in this chapter.

walk to the ground, passing en route the electric unit depot, the engine shed entrance and quite a substantial brick-built building belonging to British Road Services.

Once empty, the ten or twelve football-special carriages, would often be pushed by a Fratton-allocated 'C2X' class 0–6–0 or an 'E4' class 0–6–2 tank into a single siding on the north side of the Up main line just beyond Fratton Bridge (adjacent to Sydenham Terrace). This was a tricky manoeuvre as the set of carriages had to be pushed across both the Down and the Up main lines to gain access to the siding. After the match the locomotive which brought the train into Fratton would reverse into the siding and couple up to the carriages. With a 3.00 o'clock kick-off, the return train would depart from the siding at about 5.10 p.m., giving it plenty of time to get back to the station and pick up the away team supporters on Platform 1.

Apart from the usual local and cross-country steam workings another type of train frequented Portsmouth in July and August particularly – the holiday special. These would not normally stop at Fratton but pass through on platforms 2 or 3 and terminate at Portsmouth Harbour station. It must have been a severe test for a locomotive to haul twelve carriages crammed with holiday-makers up the 1 in 61 gradient to Portsmouth and Southsea (High Level). The sight of a holiday special appearing round the curve north of Fratton station was always greeted with shouts of glee, for it could be quite a rare class such as a 'Britannia' or a Standard class 5 from the Midlands or North Wales. Many of these trains, however, were Western Region class 'Hall', 'Grange' and 'Manor' or even a '4300' class 2–6–0. In earlier years, if you were lucky, 'Castle' class 4–6–0s also appeared. These specials had a motley collection of headboards; they nearly always displayed a reporting code in black and white and sometimes this was chalked on the smokebox door as well.

Some of the holiday specials that I had the pleasure to jot down in my notebook as they made their way to 'Sunny Southsea' were 'Manor' 4–6–0 No. 7801 *Anthony Manor* with a train from Swindon on Sunday 5 July 1959, Battle of Britain class No. 34049 *Anti-Aircraft Command* with a 'Bristol Holiday Express' headboard on Friday 31 July 1959 and 'Hall' class 4–6–0 No. 5943 *Elmdon Hall* of Didcot depot with a headboard displaying the words 'Pressed Steel Company' – this was on Saturday 4 June 1960. Diesel-hauled holiday specials were infrequent, but on Saturday 18 June 1960 No. D5517 of Stratford depot (30A) came in with a large headboard proclaiming 'Ever Ready Batteries' – this was from the Essex area. Returning to steam, 'Hall' class 4–6–0 No. 5944 *Ickenham Hall* appeared on Saturday 5 August 1960 proudly displaying a large coloured board 'Midlands Holiday Excursion'. Many years previously there used to be an annual 'Black Cat' cigarette factory holiday special to Southsea, but in those days holiday-makers alighted at Portsmouth and Southsea (High Level) and were conveyed by special buses to Southsea Common for their accommodation, 'under canvas' near a popular tree-lined area known as Ladies' Mile.

My mother, always in a constant state of worry regarding the whereabouts of her son, even though she knew I would be around the station footbridge with my pals, often made a detour from her shopping to call in at the station footbridge 'just to check'. Once she produced a bag of six jam doughnuts which she had bought at Hick's in Fratton Road, and offered me one. As I put the cake to my mouth, five of my pals suddenly appeared and needless to say my mum's cakes were rapidly devoured – she had to return to Hick's cake shop to make another purchase. With cakes in addition to all the other attractions I've mentioned it is not surprising that we trainspotters gladly spent up to ten hours a day around the Fratton station footbridge.

Saturday 13 June 1959 is typical of many summer Saturdays spent trainspotting from the footbridge. Although I have singled out this particular day to mention some of the locomotives that were noted, I should point out that I was not at the station for the full twenty-four hours and consequently many other workings went unnoticed! 'Hall' class 4–6–0 No. 5901 *Hazel Hall* arrived at Platform 2 at 11.30 a.m. with the Monday–Saturday passenger train from Reading General. A holiday special displaying a very large blue board, its wording lost in time, was hauled by 'Hall' class 4–6–0 No. 6910 *Gossington Hall* and 'Modified Hall' class 4–6–0 No. 7920 *Coney Hall* displaying an 'X27' reporting code. Two 'Schools' class 4–4–0s were noted, No. 30905 *Tonbridge* on an excursion from Wolverhampton, which it had taken over at Basingstoke, and No. 30901 *Winchester*. Other workings included 'H15' class 4–6–0 No. 30489 of Nine Elms (70A) which came 'light', 'S15' class 4–6–0 No. 30501 on the 12.15 p.m. to Plymouth, which had departed from Portsmouth and Southsea (Low Level), and two Fratton-allocated 'U' class 2–6–0s, Nos. 31638 and 31809, both employed on local passenger trains. Other Fratton- allocated engines noted were 'M7' class 0–4–4 tank No. 30357, 'K' class 2–6–0 No. 32349 and 'C2X' class 0–6–0 No. 32548, the last mentioned being employed on carriage duties. Also noted was Maunsell-designed 'Q' class 0–6–0 No. 30544, along with a host of Standard class 4 2–6–0s including Nos 76009, 76016, 76026 and 76068.

Not to be outdone by the volume of steam operations, that particular day saw one of the famous 'Brighton Belle' Pullman units arrive at the electric unit depot, No. 3052, with carriages 87, 90 and 91, together with named carriages *Vera* and *Audrey*. To add to the daily sighting of 2-BIL, 2-HAL and 4-COR electric units in their SR green liveries, we also noted several of the aged four-carriage suburban units Nos 4376, 4515 and 4516, and newly out-shopped units from Eastleigh Carriage and Wagon Works, Nos 5602, 5603, 6029 and 6061.

Saturday 13 June 1959 was the kind of day when Fratton station footbridge was a magnet for trainspotters. Who could blame us for spending up to ten blissful hours there.

Quite often, after watching the antics of PC 'Dutchie' Holland and maybe the re-poling of a trolleybus on Fratton Bridge, we trainspotters would visit A.H. Skinner's friendly sweet shop next door to Lloyds Bank on the corner of Selbourne Terrace and Fratton Road. Here we would gaze at rows of large glass sweet jars filled with sweets of all kinds. One of my favourites was a quarter pound of Nuttall's Mintoes, but mostly we would buy, for a few pennies, a packet of Spangles, Opal Fruits or Refreshers. Sometimes we would buy a sherbet 'dab' or some lemonade powder and add this to a jug of water to make our own fizzy drink. The shop also sold bottles of lemonade, ice creams and cigarettes. The latter, I am proud to say, never appealed to me or my friends, and apart from Norman, our middle-aged trainspotter friend, I don't remember any of my friends indulging in the habit. If they did, then it was never during a railway trip or station visit.

Another source of refreshment was the small café in Goldsmith Avenue opposite the station footbridge, known as the 'Bridge Café'. The footbridge was quite cold during the winter months, and the café was handy for cups of tea and coffee. In addition, there were the attractions of a juke-box, on which I seem to remember playing the instrumental 'Tequila' by The Champs over and over again, and a pinball machine to which we were all addicted! Fruit machines were almost unheard of during our early trainspotting days. A café still exists at this location, albeit under another name.

12

A Duo of Rovers

Rail Rover tickets were very popular in my trainspotting days. The ticket-holder could choose either a Regional or an All Line ticket, for either a seven-day or, if you were ambitious, a fourteen-day period and you had the choice of first- or second-class seating. It was an ideal way to travel the railway system, not only for railway enthusiasts pursuing their hobby but also for members of the general public who wanted to visit several locations in their allotted time, especially during the summer holidays so they could visit both the countryside and the seaside. I bought Southern Region Rail Rovers in September 1959 and August 1960, as did two pals, Bill Jenkins and Jim 'Jimpy' Lawrence. We exploited the SR timetable to its fullest, consulting and double-checking departure and arrival times and allowing enough time for connections. Our eventual schedules meant that we travelled both by day and by night.

During 1959 and 1960 one could travel from London (Waterloo) to Plymouth on an overnight service and naturally we took full advantage of this facility. Although the overnight train took two or three hours longer than a normal daytime service we did not mind, as it gave us extra time for sleeping or resting after a day of intensive trainspotting. The additional time on the journey was because the train stopped at numerous stations en route to load and off-load mail and newspapers. As darkness approached, the compartment light would be dimmed, the blinds pulled down and our haversacks and duffel bags put to use as pillows. We hoped for an uninterrupted night but it did not always work out that way. On our first Rail Rover trip Jim, being of very small stature, decided to use his own method of getting a good night's kip by using the string luggage rack high above the compartment seat! He was well into the land of nod with mild bouts of snoring when a ticket collector appeared. Bill and I had to raise our voices somewhat to disguise the snoring and luckily, with Jim covered by his plastic mac, the ticket collector did not notice the extra luggage!

Our 1959 escapade took place between 5 and 11 September and our second-class ticket set us back just £6. On this, my inaugural Rail Rover, I had actually applied for and received official permits to visit most of the locomotive depots in our schedule. I took my dad's Brownie box camera, but for some reason I did not take many photographs.

At Ashford depot (73F) we saw twenty-five steam and from here we enjoyed a memorable journey to Dover steam-hauled by 'West Country' class 4–6–2 No. 34003 *Plymouth*. We made our way via the Priory station to Ramsgate and then Faversham, followed by Gillingham (Kent) to visit the rather small three-lane engine shed (73D), noting just eight steam 'on shed', including a 'Q1' 0–6–0 No. 33037. That day we were thrilled to see the famous train, The Golden Arrow, while on our way to London (Victoria). It was hauled by 'Battle of Britain' class 4–6–2 No. 34085 *501 Squadron*. It had been a day of intense travelling, clocking up almost 300 miles and the locomotives that we witnessed between our engine shed visits proved to be the highlights of a day in which we noted a total of 106 steam.

I will not attempt to describe in great detail the remaining six days of this escapade, only to say that we visited engine sheds at Eastleigh (71A), Exeter (83C), Exmouth Junction (72A), Yeovil (72C), Templecombe (82G), Tonbridge (73J), Tunbridge Wells West (75F), Barnstaple Junction (72E), Tilbury (33B), Ramsgate (73G), Dover (73H), Feltham (70B) and Hither Green (73C). Jottings in my notebook remind me that we were steam-hauled between Salisbury and Exeter Central by 'Merchant Navy' class 4–6–2 No. 35020 *Bibby Line*, between Yeovil Junction and Yeovil Town by 'M7' class 0–4–4 tank No. 30131, which was push-and-pull fitted, and while in the Kent area by Standard class 4 2–6–4 tank No. 80014 between Tonbridge and Tunbridge Wells West. In those days we had the green-liveried 'Hastings' diesel units working out of Charing Cross to the Kent seaside resorts; we were lucky to sample a ride on one between Tonbridge and Waterloo East. The lure of visiting railway stations while in London was too great to resist and some of those I recall were St Pancras, Euston and Kings Cross. At the last mentioned I noted for the first time the prototype main-line diesel-electric locomotive *Deltic*. Our visit to Tilbury in Essex was via the ferry from Gravesend in North Kent at a cost of 7*d* to cross the River Thames.

We had always felt that something might not go as planned. Towards the end of our fifth day of the Southern Region Rail Rover for some unknown reason we had diverged from our scheduled timetable. We were at Dover Priory station in the mid-evening and to get home to Portsmouth that night we had two alternatives to travel via London or via Hastings and Brighton. I did not agree with Bill and Jim's decision to travel via London, so we went our separate ways. Everything went to (the revised) plan until I reached Brighton, where I asked the ticket collector, 'When is the next train to Portsmouth?' 'Six o'clock tomorrow morning,' he replied. He suggested that I catch a local train to Worthing and Bognor Regis and try to get a connection at Barnham for Portsmouth. There was no connection at Barnham so it was down the branch line to Bognor Regis. At least, I thought, I would be able to kip in the station waiting-room overnight, but the station staff were locking up this facility shortly before midnight so I had to find alternative accommodation.

I wandered the streets and just caught a chip shop as it was about to close. I quickly devoured six pennyworth washed down with a swig of Tizer. I looked at a seafront shelter as a possible overnight bed but I was somewhat put off by the presence of tramps. Walking back towards the station I came across a large garage with numerous cars parked in its forecourt. I found an Austin 7 with a wide running board suitably sheltered by the other cars from any passing policeman, and it was here that I made my bed! The trainspotter's plastic mac, cloth cap and haversack-pillow gave me just enough comfort for an uninterrupted night's sleep. I awoke at 5.20 a.m., just as the sun was rising with the promise of another hot summer day, but I had a train to catch. The aroma from a bakery as I walked to Bognor Regis station was too good to pass. I nipped inside and bought a small loaf of bread; this was my breakfast, together with the remains of my fizzy drink from the previous day. I caught the first train out of Bognor Regis, got home and confronted my parents, and got about an hour's sleep before having to meet Bill and Jim at Fratton station and catch the 10.32 a.m. train to London.

I awoke, sufficiently recovered, to the sound of my alarm clock at 9 a.m. After a quick wash, I packed my haversack for the day ahead with the standard contents – egg sandwiches, crisps, a Hales apricot pie and a bottle of squash – and then it was off to the station. When I met Bill and Jim they had a bit of a giggle when I told them about my overnight accommodation. I had obviously made the wrong decision the previous night at Dover, as my two companions had no problems getting home.

We three indulged in numerous silly antics during the week. One such event took place while travelling on a non-corridor electric unit train at a location now lost in time. After making sure that we were the only passengers, Bill insisted that the seat cushions should all be completely removed so that we could look for any coins. It was a game on the same lines as snap. If you found a coin you would shout out loud 'Three-pence' or whatever the amount found was. You can imagine the excitement on this particular journey when Bill found a penny coin and shouted out 'Penny' loudly just as the train pulled into the station platform and a very irate passenger opened our compartment door to find all the seat cushions on the floor!

When travelling with Bill and Jim there was always a sense that something unusual or odd might happen. For example, once, while travelling on an underground train, Jim calmly approached a complete stranger, a city gentleman wearing what was then the

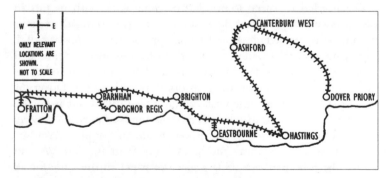

This is the evening route which I chose to take from Dover to Fratton, travelling via Canterbury West, Hastings and Eastbourne; but it only resulted in getting me as far as Bognor Regis!

standard outfit of bowler hat, suit, black shoes and tie and carrying a briefcase. 'Raise your hat, sir,' Jim said. Much to our amazement the city gent duly obliged to reveal a complete dome! We were in fits of laughter as Jim shouted out loudly, 'Dome!' ('Dome' in trainspotter's language was a bald head.) Being quite confused and bewildered by the whole affair, the gentleman replaced his bowler hat and moved further along the train; the other passengers in that carriage must have thought we were nutcases! With Jim's foolhardy antics and Bill's constant jerky stutter, I found myself between two rather off-the-wall duffelbag-carrying trainspotters, where anything that was possible might happen! Jim instigated another prank while travelling on London's tube trains. Before leaving Portsmouth, he would visit a joke shop and buy imitation 'dog's mess'. I remember him placing it very discreetly on the floor next to an elderly lady with a dog, and tapping her on the shoulder to bring it to her attention: it certainly caused her some embarrassment!

My 1960 Southern Region Rail Rover trip was also with Bill Jenkins and Jim Lawrence, and took place between Saturday 6 and Friday 12 August. It produced just as many amusing stories as the previous year – with Bill and Jim as travelling companions this was not difficult. Our ticket, which had increased from £6 to £6 10s, enabled us to travel 2,030 miles to our own schedules, some of which were very tight to say the least! We 'bunked' thirty-two engine sheds in a seven-day shed-bashing *tour de force*. We even took in some Western Region depots and of course visited some London stations and depots.

We needed to carry some kind of paperwork with us just in case we were approached by an angry foreman asking to see our permit. This was where David Copus proved to be most helpful, supplying us with a wad of used permits for the areas we intended to visit. Fortunately for us, we only had to show one of these illegal permits to a depot foreman once and this was at Dover. As I entered the yard a somewhat strident voice called out from the confines of a small nearby hut: 'Have you got your permit?' Waving the relevant 8 × 10in piece of paper in the air I replied, 'Yes, sir.' 'Mind how you go' came the quick reply from the hut. We had fooled the foreman by waving a piece of paper in the air – for all he knew it could have been a letter from my auntie!

The week had many highlights but top of the list was our visit to Taunton depot (83B) at the unearthly hour of 2.45 a.m. We had reached this section of our timetable via an overnight train from Waterloo to Exeter and Plymouth and used a small waiting-room on the centre platforms of Exeter (St David's) station, which luckily for us remained open all night. It was a trainspotter's delight, with many freight trains rumbling through the station, and we got very little sleep. It must have been around 2 a.m. that we saw a passenger and newspaper train about to depart and were told it was going to Taunton. Having no time to buy tickets, we boarded the train which was hauled by a 'Warship' class diesel.

On arrival at a rather deserted Taunton station we noticed that the exit gates from our platform were securely locked with a large padlock, or so we thought. We pushed the gates but they would not budge, so Bill and Jim decided to climb over. This proved to be quite tricky, and it took them at least five minutes. The movement of the gates as Bill and Jim climbed them caused the large padlock to become loose, so I removed the lock and to the amazement of my two pals walked casually through the open gates. Fortunately there were no railwaymen nearby to observe our antics! There were a few choice words from Bill and Jim but we had overcome this obstacle and so we made the walk to the engine shed. We must have caught the foreman sleeping as our visit was completed without seeing a soul, an eerie experience indeed – we kept expecting to hear a voice calling us, but it didn't happen. On that visit I cleared the '1366' class 0–6–0 pannier tanks with No. 1366 in a depot housing over fifty predominantly Western Region steam awaiting their respective duties for the coming day.

We also took in other Western Region locomotive depots, including Old Oak Common (81A) and Slough (81B). For the latter we were thrilled to be steam-hauled by 'Castle' class 4–6–0 No. 5098 *Clifford Castle* between Reading General and Slough.

As with the previous Rail Rover, we visited London stations and depots, including two visits to Kings Cross depot (34A). We frequently needed to travel the Underground and often found these journeys boring and uneventful. On one journey on a crowded rushhour tube train approaching Kings Cross, however, Jim took the opportunity to make use of a packet of stink bombs he had bought from a novelty shop in Portsmouth before our trip. We caused quite a commotion on that train! It certainly gave us a seat as many passengers moved as far away from the evil smell as possible!

In this action-packed week we travelled just over 2,000 miles, took some photographs and gained some amusing stories to tell our friends when we met on Fratton station footbridge the following week. We paid roughly 7*d* for every ten miles that we travelled on this Rail Rover. Just compare this with the cost of travel on the rail network today!

13

Miniatures and Ghosts

It was a regular routine of my teenage years to sit down at the table with my mum and dad for our Sunday roast dinner and then listen to 'The Billy Cotton Band Show' on the radio. If the weather was favourable, we would often take a Southdown bus from Fratton Road to the Hilsea district of Portsmouth and alight at Hilsea Lido, a popular spot just south of Portscreek. Here we would have the pleasure of travelling behind a steam locomotive on the Hilsea Miniature Railway. This little-known miniature railway tucked away in a corner of Portsmouth was an added attraction for the children using the adjacent open-air swimming pools. It began its life in the late 1940s and lasted until the early 1950s before it was closed.

The single-line railway ran alongside the boating lake at Hilsea Lido and curved round on an embankment following the north-east shoreline of Portsmouth Harbour to a point near Alexandra Park, providing a round trip of nearly a mile hauled by a Pacific type steam engine named *Robin Hood* based on an LNER 'A1' class. The carriages were constructed of wood and were open-topped. A turntable was situated at each end of the line, an engine and carriage shed was provided and a very basic station existed at Hilsea, of which the concrete platform is still *in situ* today. Apart from the embankment and the platform there are no other signs of the railway but the steam locomotive still survives somewhere in the north of England.

Another popular miniature railway was the Southsea Miniature Railway, located near the promenade at Southsea between Clarence Pier and South Parade Pier. Its position left it open to all the elements, although a sturdy concrete wall partly protected it from the ravages of Spithead. The SMR was in an ideal position to attract children from the nearby beach. Not only was it popular with the local children and their parents but it was also a major attraction for holiday-makers and tourists, being prominently advertised for many years in the official holiday guide to Portsmouth and Southsea.

As a trainspotter and steam railway enthusiast I was naturally drawn to any form of steam-operated railway and the attraction of this 10¼in-gauge line on my doorstep was no exception. I was lucky enough to make contact with a Mr Hinks, who gave up his spare time during the summer weekends to drive and fire steam engines Nos 1002 *Valiant* and 1003 *Victory* on the SMR. I met him through going to school with his son, and this resulted in a few free journeys! The line ran for nearly three-quarters of a mile and it included a balloon loop, a tunnel (which in fact was a 20yd section of an old Anderson air-raid shelter, covered in earth), a sizeable engine shed and workshop. The railway closed in 1989, after which it became the target of vandalism by unruly youths with nothing better to do with their time. Sadly, the SMR has been wiped from the scene.

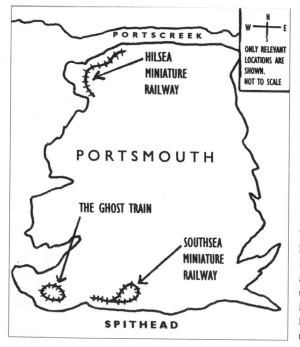

These are the locations of the Hilsea Miniature Railway, the Southsea Miniature Railway and the Ghost Train.

Once it had gone the area first emerged as a Sea Life Centre, and today the Blue Reef Aquarium occupies the location along with a grassed bandstand area. The closure of this miniature railway was a shame, as the lineside ornaments and gardens that graced the area were a prominent feature and enjoyed by everyone. I especially recall the stone statue of Harold Wilson, complete with pipe, that stood beside the track. As with the Hilsea Miniature Railway, the steam engines have moved on to be used at other locations in Great Britain.

A completely different source of fun and adventure for me and my teenage pals was Billy Manning's Fun Fair and Amusement Park next to Clarence Pier, Southsea. Here we would ride the dodgem cars and the big wheel, and get absolutely shaken up with a ride on the waltzer, guaranteed to make you throw up – I should have known better than to partake of a hotdog followed by candy floss before the ride! When we were in a more relaxed mood we would play the pin-ball machines, giggle at the then somewhat naughty 'What the Butler Saw' machine, put a penny in the 'Laughing Policeman' and take home with us a printed metal strip with our name on it from the printing machine. Our favourite attraction, however, apart from chatting up numerous young ladies, was, much to the annoyance of its operator, a ride on the ghost train.

We had devised a meticulous plan. We usually travelled in a group of three or four and made sure we were the only passengers on the slow-moving train. When the train entered the dimly lit and spooky area with ghosts and cobwebs dangling from the ceiling, we would carefully alight from the carriage. The empty train would then return to the starting point, and a very annoyed operator would have to travel back into the darkness with his torch to look for us! It was part of our plan that we also would carry a torch with a powerful beam and when the operator appeared with his torch we would direct our own torch into his eyes, dazzling him. Then we would smartly nip on to the train and with some very deft footwork make a hasty retreat into the funfair crowds! After repeating this antic on numerous occasions, the operator became wise to us, so we would wear cloth caps and sunglasses to disguise our identity! It was all great fun, but that operator must have cursed us whenever we rode the ghost train.

14

London, a 17-Hour Day

Living only about 70 miles away, naturally we visited London quite frequently, mostly for trainspotting but also for quite a few social events such as pop concerts – although even these were combined with visits to railway stations. My railway visits to the capital usually took place on a Saturday or a Sunday and the advantage of the latter was that the engine sheds would be crammed with locomotives awaiting their respective duties for the coming week, the perfect situation for any trainspotter. In the summer months one could note visiting engines that had brought holiday excursions from the north of England or the Midlands, and during the football season steam locomotives from Lancashire, Yorkshire or further afield used on football excursions.

As already mentioned, we trainspotters from Fratton favoured an early start to our day and so we would nearly always catch the 5.32 a.m. 'workman's' electric unit train from Fratton to Waterloo – except on a Sunday, when it was a 6.08 a.m. departure on the ordinary service train. We would set our alarm clocks for around 4.45 a.m. and, most importantly, pack our haversacks, duffel bags and satchels with the necessary clothing and ample food and drink. After a relaxing journey we would arrive at about 7.50 a.m., ready for an intense programme that would see us visit anything between seven and eleven engine sheds and many main-line stations.

Our areas to visit ranged from Slough in the west, Norwood Junction in the south-east and Hornsey in the north to Plaistow in the east. Obviously, countless miles of travel were involved, mostly by tube and suburban trains, but buses and taxis were frequently called upon too, not to mention the numerous miles by shanks's pony. At the end of a long day's travelling in London we would usually catch the 8.50 p.m. electric unit train home to Portsmouth via Guildford and Haslemere and by our return to Fratton we would have clocked up a seventeen-hour day!

We carried with us a selection of used permits relating to London motive power depots. These were in the hands of David Copus and we felt confident that these second-hand pieces of paper would fool the shed foreman if ever the situation arose. Fortunately for us, it only happened on a few visits. You can imagine what was going through our minds as the official tried to read the partly obliterated date – our story was that the permit had had a drink spilt on it! Usually, however, we would try to evade the foreman. We also had to take extreme caution to avoid falling into inspection pits, look out for oily walkways and, most importantly, be wary of moving locomotives. If we had achieved all this, and had taken some photographs and made some references on locomotives noted in our books, then it was deemed that we had successfully 'bunked' another engine shed! Regarding the used permits, it is worth mentioning that in those days we did not have access to photocopying machines.

What was perhaps my most memorable London visit, however, was one weekday in 1960. Eleven engine sheds and seven stations were crammed into the day, in the company of David Copus and four other enthusiasts. We caught the 'workman's' train as usual, which afforded us a cheap way of travel. Tickets were only issued for a certain number of miles from the issuing station, which meant officially that we had to leave the train either at Petersfield or Esher to renew our ticket to Waterloo. This we never did, as by that stage of the journey the train would be crammed tight with commuters! We were never queried by any ticket inspector.

The table below shows the eleven depots in order of visit and the totals of steam and diesel locomotives 'on shed'.

Visit	Depot/Code		Steam	Diesel
1	Stewarts Lane (73A)		37	4
2	Finsbury Park (FP)	–	19	
3	Hornsey (34B)		44	6
4	Stratford (30A)		126	85
5	Old Oak Common (81A)		119	14
6	Willesden (1A)		96	13
7	Neasden (14D)		44	2

Visit	Depot/Code	Steam	Diesel
8	Cricklewood (14A)	50	13
9	Camden (1B)	37	19
10	Kentish Town (14B)	55	4
11	Hither Green (73C)	22	17

We pushed ourselves to the limit, only eating and drinking while travelling between locations. We were weary and tired but happy when we reached Waterloo at the end of the day and looked forward to the luxury of our journey home to Portsmouth in a twelve-carriage 4-COR electric unit.

That weekday in 1960 we noted 637 different BR steam locomotives and probably the most unusual sighting was a 'Q1' class from the Southern Region 'on shed' at Stratford, No. 33013 of Feltham (70B).

During other London visits we came across numerous oddities at the depots we visited, such as an 'H16' class 4–6–2 tank from the Southern Region in Cricklewood roundhouse, and a pair of preserved locomotives at Old Oak Common, No. 3440 *City of Truro* and Caledonian Railway 4–4–2 No. 123. Hither Green depot (73C) was host to many Eastern Region 'J17' class and 'J50' class 0–6–0 tanks; these would be used on transfer freight trains between North London and the extensive marshalling yard at Hither Green in south-east London. Nine Elms depot (70A) had from the early 1960s as replacements for the ageing 'M7' 0–4–4 tanks, an influx of ex-Great Western 0–6–0 pannier tanks – on one of my visits in September 1960 I noted Nos 4634, 4672, 4698 and 9770.

15

Play Up Pompey!

My passion for Portsmouth Football Club began on Saturday 26 February 1949 when I attended Fratton Park for the very first time. What an occasion it proved to be! Our visitors were Derby County in the FA Cup Sixth Round. I remember vividly having to stand on a wooden box situated at the rear of the north terrace so that I could see; I was then only eight years old. We won 2–1 with Ike Clarke scoring both goals and this was in the presence of a fantastic attendance of 51,385. I did not realise it at the time, but that was a record crowd that will never be surpassed – and I was there: 'Play Up Pompey!'

One of our pastimes in the 1960s was to keep ourselves fit. This was partly achieved by lengthy walks around the streets of Portsmouth and Southsea, which not only prepared us for our energy-sapping trainspotting trips but also kept us in trim for our Sunday Football League matches. We often had a kick-about at Kingston Recreation Ground or Bransbury Park using jumpers for goal-posts. We used a large red plastic ball but it was prone to bursting – and repair kits never seemed to work! These balls were lighter than a full-size football and cost about 3s 6d (about 18p). On a warm evening, training would continue until sunset. Apart from this we would sometimes run through the beach shingle between South Parade Pier and Eastney to build up our leg muscles – especially before the start of a new football season.

A Bizarre Object Emerges

Early in 1960 in the course of one of our long walks, in this case through Old Portsmouth, David Copus chanced to spot a large brass dinner gong displayed in an antiques shop window in Queen Street.

He urged me to find out its cost. A few minutes later I had made a decision which would affect our trainspotting and football excursion trips for many years to come. I purchased that heavy dinner gong for the sum of £1! Before I entered the shop we held a discussion in which David suggested, with our full agreement, that a dinner gong painted in Portsmouth FC colours with 'Pompey' displayed on its face could be taken into Fratton Park and used to accompany our vocal support. It seemed a unique way of demonstrating our presence. We positioned ourselves at the rear of the old Fratton End stand and whenever Pompey scored a goal or made a good move, we gave the gong a few hearty bashes. After a bit of commotion and a few moans and groans from nearby supporters, people eventually became used to the incessant bashing and the 'Pompey' gong became accepted as part of the football scene. My dad had made me a very strong gong stick out of beech wood, and this and the gong still survive today.

This bizarre object was first publicly 'blooded' at Fratton Park, but its appearances increased dramatically in the 1960s when I decided to take the gong on the club's football excursions to such places as Cardiff, Birmingham, Ipswich and Bristol, to name but a few. Naturally it was taken to nearly every London ground, but one that it definitely did not visit, for obvious reasons, was The Dell, home of our close rivals, Southampton FC.

The gong weighed about seven pounds, and the question that always cropped up was 'Who's going to take turns in carrying it?' Knowing that whenever we travelled on football excursions with the gong we would visit some engine sheds or stations before the match, I took an especially strong plastic carrier bag, which proved an ideal holder for the heavy brass gong.

On one such visit to Cardiff in 1963 David Copus, Roy Davidson and I were 'bunking' Radyr depot (88B) before seeing the game at Ninian Park. David had been designated to carry the gong around Radyr. All seemed well until just before our departure from the depot, when David took his revenge on an innocent elderly railway worker by quietly creeping up behind him and unleashing four or five hefty bashes on the gong. The worker, in a state of confusion, was heard to exclaim, 'What's going on?' Fortunately for us we had completed our visit; staff suddenly appeared from doors and faces appeared at windows. The offending object was quickly put back in the bag and we made a smart exit!

It was on this visit to Radyr in September 1963 that we saw main-line diesel locomotives making inroads into South Wales, resulting in many Great Western steam locomotives of the 0–6–2 side tank and 0–6–0 pannier tank designs being laid up for storage and eventual scrap. We noted that the 'dead line' contained just four steam, Nos 3406, 4289, 5608 and 6607. There were a further twenty-six steam 'on shed' but for many of them their days were numbered.

The Pompey gong was taken into Ninian Park and we mingled with the home supporters who were quite amazed to see such a novel way of support. In fact a nearby group of Cardiff City fans commented on our originality and we struck up a conversation in which I mentioned that the gong was widely travelled. On this particular visit my team went home 2–1 winners – I wonder if the gong helped?

Our return fare to Cardiff on that day was 27s 6d, and we were steam-hauled between Portsmouth and Salisbury by Standard class 5 4–6–0 No. 73119 and between Salisbury and Cardiff General by 'Hall' class 4–6–0 No. 6953 *Leighton Hall*. The same two locomotives were used on the return excursion.

During one of our many rail visits to London football grounds, our group of fourteen youths visited locomotive depots at Hither Green (73C) and Norwood Junction (75C) before making our way to Selhurst Park where Crystal Palace were playing Portsmouth. That Saturday afternoon we were part of a crowd of 30,000 people and for us Pompey supporters it was a memorable game for several reasons; our team won by a 3–0 scoreline, and when the referee blew the final whistle thousands of Pompey supporters, including us, swarmed onto the pitch to congratulate the players. David Copus was holding the gong at head height in front of him and, constantly bashing it and running towards the players, was unaware that he was heading directly towards the referee. The gong caught the ref a glancing blow on the back of his head and he crumpled to the ground! We stood motionless for a few seconds while he gingerly regained his feet looking rather dazed. Seeing that he had recovered sufficiently, we very quickly melted back into the crowd and out of the ground. When reading the report on the match in the paper the next day, we were taken aback to read the line, 'At the end of the game hundreds of jubilant Pompey supporters rushed onto the pitch but the celebrations were somewhat marred when the match referee was felled from behind by a heavy object'!

Play Up Pompey

Not only were football excursion trains laid on to take Portsmouth supporters to away matches but also for visiting supporters attending Fratton Park – most of these had the added attraction of a buffet or restaurant car. One particularly notable occasion for spotting incoming excursions was when my team were drawn at home against Peterborough United in the Third Round of the FA Cup on Saturday 7 January 1961. We saw an incredible *seven* 'special' trains! They all terminated at Fratton station's Platform 3 between 12.30 and 2 p.m. and no doubt the signalman at the adjacent Fratton West signal-box must have found himself quite overworked. To add to this, an eighth 'special' arrived and terminated at Platform 3 steam-hauled by 'West Country' class 4–6–2 No. 34105 *Swanage*, displaying a gigantic headboard on its smokebox door proclaiming 'Westbury Panto Excursion'. This train's passengers were mostly children, off to sample the pantomime at the King's Theatre in Albert Road, Southsea.

Returning to the football excursions, of which I photographed a selection, the locomotives employed were 'Hall' class 4–6–0s Nos 4921 *Eaton Hall* (reporting code X56) and 6927 *Lilford Hall*, 'Modified Hall' class 4–6–0 No. 6970 *Whaddon Hall* (reporting code X57) and four 'West Country' class 4–6–2s, Nos 34017 *Ilfracombe*, 34020 *Seaton*, 34037 *Clovelly* and 34045 *Ottery St Mary*. That early afternoon was indeed a trainspotter's delight, and apart from the eight special trains we had the usual service trains such as the arrival from Reading General hauled by 'Modified Hall' class 4–6–0 No. 7906 *Fron Hall*, a selection of 'U' class 2–6–0s and a variety of Standard class 4 2–6–0s and 5 class 4–6–0s, which were all seen from the station footbridge.

The incoming specials must have made a considerable impact on the match attendance that afternoon as the gate was 27,533. Unfortunately, if you were a Pompey fan, the final score read Portsmouth 1, Peterborough United 2. I recall the legendary Jimmy Dickinson wearing the No. 6 shirt that day and another long-serving stalwart, Alex Wilson, scoring the Portsmouth goal. For us Portsmouth fans that season went from bad to worse, ending with Portsmouth being relegated to Division 3!

The Midlands seemed to be the limit for travelling Portsmouth supporters on these excursions but I remember one exception in the

1965–66 season, when a train was laid on to take fans to Carlisle. I did not participate in this journey but unfortunately those that did had to return home feeling rather dejected as we lost 2–1.

After watching our idols at Fratton Park on a Saturday afternoon, we then attempted to emulate them by playing in the City of Portsmouth Sunday Football League. My own experiences at this level spread over nineteen seasons and I finally played my last game at King George's Field, Cosham when I was forty-four years old. I still retain my old leather football boots as a memento! I have to admit that I was never going to be a star player, although when playing in my favourite position on the right wing in a number 7 shirt I did try to model myself on my Pompey idol, Peter Harris. I was never one of the regulars on the team. It did not worry me too much as Sunday was always an ideal day to travel and visit engine sheds.

There were various opportunities for playing football at Grosvenor Press. Mostly I played for the 'A' and 'B' teams, but my colleague and friend Paul Bailey used to organise two teams to play 'friendlies', for the benefit of players who could not command a place in the first team. These teams rejoiced in the print-related names of Caxton United FC and Rockwell FC – William Caxton was the first English printer (after whom a type font was named) and Rockwell is another type font, designed in 1910. Rather than taking things too seriously we played football for fun and enjoyment and of course a visit to the pub afterwards! I recall that one particular 'friendly' with a 10.30 a.m. kick-off was against a team from London who were touring the Hampshire area. We lost that match 31–0 – the fact that our team had been to a nightclub the previous night and were full of ale probably accounts for the scoreline!

Surprisingly, I did not join a Sunday league team by the name of Ferndale although I did 'guest' for them a few times when they were desperate for players! Eddie Rooke, David Copus and at least four other railway enthusiasts played in the tangerine shirts of Ferndale FC. David came across this name visiting engine sheds in South Wales, Ferndale being a sub-depot of Treherbert (88F). The story goes back to the late 1950s when David, as Secretary, suggested on returning from South Wales that their newly-formed City of Portsmouth Sunday Football League team be called Ferndale – and thus the name was born. David and Eddie were both involved in forming this team, and many railway enthusiasts who feature in this book also played for Ferndale FC. A team photograph appears in the plate section. Ferndale FC holds the City of Portsmouth Sunday League goal scoring record of 37–0 – perhaps the gruelling training sessions played a part!

Steam-hauled football excursions enabled us railway enthusiasts to visit locations we would not have normally visited on Sunday excursions and day trips, but with the demise of BR steam power in the mid-1960s, such excursions were gradually becoming diesel-hauled – by the end of the 1960s we even saw double-decker buses and coaches being used for this facility.

A football special was run from Portsmouth Harbour to Stoke-on-Trent on Saturday 4 January 1964 on the occasion that Portsmouth were drawn away to Stoke City in the FA Cup Third Round. I went with David Copus and Frank Allen, and a host of younger enthusiasts.

The return fare was 37*s* 6*d*. The forward journey was interesting in that we had three steam locomotives from different regions hauling our buffet car excursion – Southern Region 'West Country' class 4–6–2 No. 34037 *Clovelly*, Western Region 'Modified Hall' class 4–6–0 No. 7920 *Coney Hall* and LMS class 5 4–6–0 No. 45392.

David brought with him on this trip an amended permit to visit Stoke depot (5D), but I don't think even that would have impressed the shed foreman if he caught us on this foggy afternoon feeling our way around the shed and yard in conditions that were hazardous to say the least! For some reason I decided to take photographs in these conditions, probably with the thought of producing an eerie effect. While in the yard area I saw 'Jinty' 0–6–2 tanks Nos 47628 and 47664 suddenly appear out of the mist and expected one of the drivers to give us a telling off. Luckily we completed our visit safely. Seeing the match at the Victoria Ground was less memorable: our beloved Pompey were beaten 4–1. An advert in the match programme (price 6*d*) told us a packet of Park Drive would cost 3*s* 5*d*.

In 1967 a double-decker bus took us (David Copus, Roger Emptage and four others) all the way from Portsmouth to Derby for a league match at the Baseball Ground. Not only was the transport different but so was the scoreline, Portsmouth beating Derby County 1–0 with George Smith scoring. The Pompey gong was taken on this trip and I recall the home fans marvelling at its unique use. As at most home and away matches we also saw the Pompey mascot, a certain Barry Harris. Suitably attired in a sailor's uniform complete with cap, he was carrying a placard around the ground displaying the words 'Play Up Pompey', and when he came to where the Portsmouth fans were gathered he would encourage much vocal support. It was all good, clean fun and at no time did it provoke any violence or abuse in the crowd. For the record, it cost us just 4s for admission to the terraces! In 1968 I had the dubious pleasure of travelling the long journey by coach from Fratton Park to Huddersfield Town's ground, Leeds Road, where I witnessed a dour 0–0 draw.

Labels Unlimited!

The football excursion trains from Portsmouth were extremely popular, and enabled us to give the Pompey gong an airing at most of our opponents' grounds. Another part of our plans was a small piece of paper with the legend 'Play Up Pompey' proudly printed upon it in royal blue ink. The idea came from David Copus and, believe it or not, two batches of 2,500 of these 4 × 3in gummed labels were printed. Since I worked at the local printers, these labels were readily available! The initial intention was to stick these in obvious places in opponents' grounds as a reminder to the home fans of our visit. They were duly plastered all over the terraces, stanchions, walls and even in the gents! But as the years progressed these labels were spread more widely. They were now being off-loaded at every conceivable location on the way to the home football ground – at fish and chip shops, telephone kiosks, post-boxes, on lampposts and, it goes without saying, on London Transport underground trains and buses!

Not content to restrict the gummed label phenomenon to football excursions, we also distributed them to fellow trainspotters who were Portsmouth FC fans. They in their turn spread the message of our team the length and breadth of the British Railways system. In 1962 these labels reached the far north of Scotland and a 'Welcome to Wick' road sign came in for a considerable plastering, as did Aberdeen, the ferries of the Western Isles and the city of Newcastle!

Two football excursions to Ipswich in 1964 and 1967 respectively are memorable not only for their dismal scorelines, but also for what we did with our stickers. On Saturday 7 November 1964 our beloved club somehow contrived to embarrass their supporters by losing 7–0! Naturally our group of trainspotters, which included David Copus, Roger Emptage, Peter Walsh and

Jim Davidson among others, felt somewhat depressed at the end of the match. On returning to Ipswich station we indulged in a spot of trainspotting, but at this time steam in the East Anglia area was at a premium and consequently we only noted a few diesels. The five of us adjourned to the station buffet and while sipping his tea in a crowded and noisy buffet David realised he had about 200 'Play up Pompey' labels to dispose of. We decided to give him a hand. About fifteen minutes later when we departed from the buffet, those gummed labels had been stuck securely on nearly everything in sight, including tables, chairs, floors, walls, cups, saucers, cutlery and even windows and curtains! After the crowds had dispersed the buffet proprietor and staff must have cursed our actions – it would have taken considerable elbow-grease to remove the offending pieces of paper. On Saturday 25 March 1967 we were on our second batch of 2,500 gummed labels. Poor old Pompey had been beaten again, but this time by a more respectable scoreline of 4–2. Fortunately for the staff of Ipswich station buffet, we had not allowed ourselves enough time for a second visit and they must

A 'Play Up Pompey' gummed label. There were 5,000 of these printed, approximately 4 x 3in, in royal blue ink. They were a constant source of amusement for us during the 1960s.

have been pleasantly relieved that there was no repetition of our previous actions: That's not to say that the station platform seat and porter's trolley didn't come in for some attention, though.

Perhaps the most amusing incident occurred just before our train departed. David noticed that a member of the station staff had left his up-turned peak cap on a seat. Without hesitation a gummed label was duly affixed over the porter's badge! As we boarded the train bound for Liverpool Street we were all in fits of laughter as a porter slammed our door shut. He had, unbeknown to him, a 'Play Up Pompey' label displayed on the front of his cap!

The gummed labels were an endless source of amusement wherever we travelled, whether on a football excursion or an ordinary day trip trainspotting, and I suppose we could be classed as being the original graffiti artists. Were we the forerunners of the disgraceful defacings of today that are so common over the majority of our modern railway system and living environment? Personally, I don't think so, as our actions in the 1960s were never intended to deface or cause too much hardship to anyone.

For the record, we travelled to Ipswich via Guildford to Waterloo, and then took the tube to Liverpool Street. On passing the shed at Guildford we noted Standard class '3' 2–6–0 No. 77014 which was an exile from the North-east of England because of dieselisation in that area. This locomotive had numerous allocations in its short life with BR including Blaydon, Blyth, Thornaby, Stourton and Northwich. We were diesel-hauled between Liverpool Street and Ipswich by Type 4 D1772 and on the return journey by another of the same class, D1768, both locomotives being allocated to Stratford depot (30A).

16

Eight Days on the Rails

Having undertaken Southern Region Rail Rovers in 1959 and 1960, I now had the urge for more and was contemplating greater things. During April and May in 1961 I drew up the initial plans with my close friends Eddie Rooke and Tony 'Inky' Ingram for a seven-day Western Region Rail Rover. Before this adventure we had sensibly sent off for and received most of the forty-five locomotive depot and three workshop permits needed for our visits. Nothing was left to chance: we made numerous visits to Portsmouth and Southsea railway station information office to check and double-check that our schedule was correct, with ample time for connections. Did overnight trains have seating for passengers? Would there be any engineering works? All these aspects had to be accounted for to give us a clear path ahead. We had decided to travel on a second-class All Stations ticket costing us £9 10s, from Saturday 27 May to Friday 2 June: This ticket had no restrictions, and you could travel twenty-four hours a day on all timetabled trains, including any advertised excursions – we intended to use this facility to its fullest!

Day 1: Fratton–Paddington

We left Fratton on Friday 26 May on the 7.24 p.m. electric-unit train to London (Waterloo), then went to Paddington station to collect our Rail Rover tickets. As we had time on our hands before our 12.45 a.m. departure from Paddington, Eddie suggested that we 'bunk' Old Oak Common shed. Unfortunately we met a rather irate foreman as we entered the building and were instantly ejected. Undaunted by this rare failure we hopped on a trolleybus to Acton where we whiled away some time on the pinball machines. The machines that

A trainspotters' paradise – just look at those contented teenagers with their notebooks and Biros, a scene that epitomises what trainspotting was really like in the 1960s. The location is Southampton Central station, and the date is Saturday 27 July 1963. Steam locomotives awaiting their respective departures are left, Standard class '4' 2–6–0 No. 76017 on a Cardiff to Portsmouth train, and 'West Country' class 4–6–2 No. 34105 *Swanage* on a Bournemouth to Birkenhead train. By pure coincidence, both of these locomotives have been preserved on the Mid-Hants Watercress Line in Hampshire.

The author (left) with one of his former train-spotting companions, Frank Allen, pictured at Stratford-on-Avon station in front of 'West Country' class 4–6–2 No. 34016 *Bodmin* during its visit from the Mid-Hants Railway on a Daylight Rail Tour on 8 September 2001.

The Brownie box camera that my late father purchased in 1926 was used to capture this rather delightful scene in August 1929 in Martha Street, Portsmouth. It shows my father (right) about to set off with two of his pals on one of their many cycling adventures, on this occasion to Plymouth. Cycling in those days was a pleasure as traffic was minimal – my father's destinations, usually on long weekend trips, included Somerset, Chester, Kendal, Leicester and even Newcastle. Perhaps I inherited my spirit of adventure, albeit on trains, from my father.

In the mid-1950s 'T9' class 4–4–0 No. 30732 (allocated to Fratton depot) departs from Cosham station with a Cardiff General to Portsmouth and Southsea passenger train. The 'T9' would have taken over from a Western Region locomotive at Salisbury, and travelled via Romsey and Southampton Central. Between 1970 and 1978 the author lived only yards away from where this photograph was taken. *(Graham Scott)*

A Portsmouth to Cardiff passenger train hauled by an unidentified 'T9' class 4–4–0 is about to pass under Milton Lane footbridge in 1958. This view, with the backs of the houses in Byerley Road in the background, is virtually unchanged today.

Fratton station footbridge, where my trainspotting began in earnest, summer 1960. The locomotive is a Standard class 4 2–6–0 No. 76063 of Eastleigh. The driver is seen in conversation with the Fratton West signal-box operator.

This 'H15' class 4–6–0 No. 30331, allocated to Salisbury depot (72B), was 'on shed' on my very first visit to Eastleigh depot (71A) in the company of Eddie Rooke. I photographed it at the coaling stage on Wednesday August 24 1955.

Fratton goods depot with its familiar zigzag roof is depicted in this photograph which I took in 1962. Note the interesting guard's van (left) coupled to a breakdown crane. The locomotive is a Bulleid-designed 'Q1' class 0–6–0 No. 33019.

GWR 'Hall' class locomotives were common visitors to Fratton depot, many employed on excursions. Here we see '4900' class 4–6–0 No. 5944 *Ickenham Hall* with a 'X12' reporting code and an 84F shed-plate (Stourbridge), which indicated to us trainspotters the origin of the excursion.

Eddie and I had a 'favourite' Fratton-allocated locomotive, this Stroudley-designed class 'E1' 0–6–0 tank No. 32694 of 1874 vintage. It is seen here at Fratton East in the mid-1950s. No. 32694 was a regular performer on the twice-daily goods train between Fratton goods sidings and Portsmouth Royal Naval Dockyard. Sadly, it was cut up for scrap in the early 1960s. *(Eric Grace)*

In the mid-1970s a recession hit the printing industry, and Grosvenor Press were put on a three-day working week. This was a platform for Alf Irish to display a large Union Jack in the examination papers room, nicknamed by Alf the 'Yampy room'. Alf is seen here looking rather subdued.

Women to my left and women to my right! In happier times – a refreshment stop at the Wooden Bridge public house, near Guildford, during the annual 1965 works outing to London. One of the parked coaches was ours. From left to right: Jean Moore, Susan Reid, Michael Harvey, Shirley Tidy and Valerie Peach. *(David Neil)*

Ryde Depot (70H): a typical shed scene, captured on 1 August 1963, during a 'Round the Island' coach tour with my parents. Alighting from the coach at the top of the High Street on returning to Ryde, we made the short walk to the depot. My mum and dad were sufficiently thirsty for me to lead them to a public house to consume several glasses of Mackeson – while I 'bunked' the nearby engine shed! The class 'O2' 0–4–4 tank is No. 22 *Brading*.

Above: Fratton Depot: at the date of our visit to the Royal Albert Hall, July 1964, the Roundhouse and Yard was host to many steam locomotives pending preservation – in later years preservation societies purchased some of these ex-BR steam locomotives and returned them to working order. This class 'M7' 0-4-4 tank No. 30133, with tarpaulin over its chimney, was not so lucky. It was towed away to Eastleigh Works for scrap.

Below: The Sunday excursions from Portsmouth all traversed the Cosham, Portchester, Fareham route. This early 1960s photograph depicts a 'U' class 2–6–0 engine No. 31800 at Fareham station with an east-bound parcels train. *(Sam Savage)*

Havenstreet, on the Isle of Wight Steam Railway, stages a Steam Extravaganza every August bank holiday in a field adjacent to the station. This picture was taken in 1978, with my sons, Adrian (top) aged 6 and Simon aged 2½, proudly posing in front of steam-roller FX 7034. I encouraged both of them to take an interest in steam and vintage transport, but it was not to be – their interests soon turned to other attractions.

Above: Banbury depot (84C) was also 'bunked' along with Oxford (81F) and Reading (81D) on Sunday 2 April 1961. Banbury saw twenty-six steam and six 0–6–0 diesel shunters 'on shed', including this '5100' class Prairie tank No. 5167. *(D.K. Jones Collection).*

Below: Eddie Rooke appears to be standing inside the chimney of withdrawn '4500' class 2–6–2 tank locomotive No. 5547 outside Barry Works. Its shed plate has already been removed. This photograph was taken during one of our many Sunday excursions to Cardiff in the early 1960s.

Above: Class '8F' 2–8–0 No. 48297 (3A) employed on a freight. The location is probably Bushbury.
Below: Stourbridge Junction depot (84F) – '5100' class 2–6–2 tank No. 4146.

Above: An unidentified 'Royal Scot' class 4–6–0 on a passenger train. I think the location is Bushbury.

Left: I took this photograph of a jovial group of our younger trainspotters with whom David Copus was closely associated. The location is at the entrance to Fratton station and the date is the summer of 1960. David is at the top. Putting names to the other faces is not easy after forty or so years, but they included Roy Wiltshire, Mike Dooley and Mike Chapman. The backs of the terraced houses in Walmer Road form the background. The cars in the background would be collectors items today!

Kings Cross depot (34A) This was a typical 'top shed' scene which greeted us as we successfully 'bunked' the shed at 5.40 a.m. – there were ninety-five steam locomotives crammed into the yard and depot. Left to right: 'A1' class 4–6–2 No. 60150 *Willbrook*, 'A4' class 4–6–2s Nos 60010 *Dominion of Canada*, 60007 *Sir Nigel Gresley*, and 'V2' class 2–6–2 No. 60880.

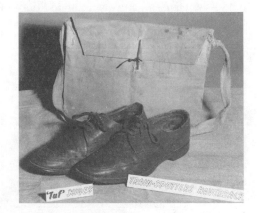

This is the haversack that I took and these are the Tuf shoes that I wore during my thirteen years of trainspotting.

These three essential reference books were carried in our haversacks on virtually every major trainspotting trip. *(Covers reproduced by permission of Ian Allan Publishing. All rights reserved.)*

Trolleybuses were a pollution-free mode of transport, and we trainspotters often travelled on them between Fratton and Portsmouth city centre or the Harbour station. Here we see bus No. 237 in the Guildhall Square in 1960. The Sussex Hotel (right) was a public house of ill repute. Note the Austin Seven car parked outside. Part of Portsmouth and Southsea High Level station can be seen above the trolleybus on the left. Sadly, the last trolleybus ran in Portsmouth in 1963. *(John Kinchen)*

This was a typical Fratton depot yard scene, which we local trainspotters knew so well. The locomotive is a Billinton design 'K' class 2–6–0 No. 32345, quietly awaiting its next turn of duty. The roundhouse building forms the background of this summer 1950 view. At this date Fratton depot had two 'K' class locomotives in its allocation, Nos 32337 and 32349.

'The footbridge of delight' – Fratton station footbridge is prominent in this photograph which I took in the summer of 1960. The locomotive is an ex-works Standard class 4 2–6–4 tank No. 80094 returning 'light' to shed. This part of Goldsmith Avenue was a popular location for taking photographs.

This photograph, which I took in the summer of 1959 from Goldsmith Avenue, shows Fratton bridge with Lloyds Bank on the corner of Selbourne Terrace and the sweet shop of A.H. Skinner next door; the trolleybus wires can be seen (top left). The locomotive is '6959' class (Modified Hall) 4–6–0 No. 7920 *Coney Hall* being reversed 'light' to Fratton depot, hence the backward glance of the driver.

Although 'bunked' many times on half-day visits from Fratton, Eastleigh depot was nevertheless included in our 1959 Southern Region Rail Rover. Tank engines dominate the scene, with (left) 'E4' class 0–6–2 No. 32506, in company with three 'M7' class 0–4–4s.

I captured this shot of Bulleid-designed 'Battle of Britain' class 4–6–2 No. 34089 *602 Squadron* during the 1960 Southern Region Rail Rover. The unmistakable chalk background tells you that the location is Dover.

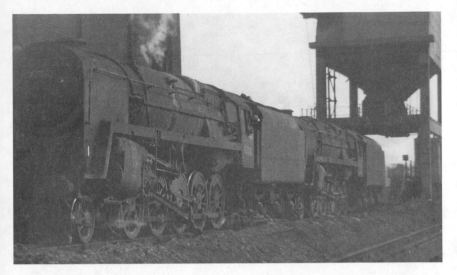

Neasden depot (14D): this was the scene that greeted us as we successfully 'bunked' the depot on the weekday trip described in chapter 14. Two '9F' class 2–10–0s, Nos 92052 and 92118, had just arrived for coal and water. My request to 'cab' No. 92052 was granted. Note the immense coaling plant.

Saturday 7 January 1961. This is one of the seven football excursions from Peterborough of which I photographed four. Locomotive is 'Modified Hall' class 4–6–0 No. 6970 *Whaddon Hall* (Reporting code X57) departing from Platform 3 at Fratton; the football supporters have been off-loaded. The lady with her baby in the pram, about to cross the main railway tracks unassisted, must have been taking some risks. Usually in those days a member of the station staff would help!

The Pompey gong and stick, purchased by the author for the sum of £1 in 1960. It was constantly aired to add to our vocal support for Portsmouth FC, not only at Fratton Park but at numerous away grounds. It is still in use today, albeit only at the author's slide show and talk when 'Diaries of a Trainspotter' is being shown.

The all-green kit of Rockwell Football Club is proudly worn by the author, pictured here at Cosham in September 1979. This was just weeks before my thirty-ninth birthday and I was still competing (or trying to) in the city of Portsmouth Sunday Football League Junior Division V.

The 'Old Emptonians' FC (named after Roger Emptage). This team photograph was taken in the early 1960s – later they became Ferndale FC. The venue is Gosport, just before playing a friendly against Cyanamid FC. Back row, left to right: Timothy Julnes, Tony 'Inky' Ingram, Terry Hunt, Eddie Rooke, Roger Emptage and Frank Allen. Front row: Adrian 'Choc' Langdown, Roger Farmer, Don Aylward, David Copus and Roy Davidson. At least six of this team were close trainspotting friends and feature prominently in this book.

A foggy day at Stoke depot (5D). This is the eerie scene that I captured in the depot yard. A 'Jinty' 0–6–2 tank, No. 47664, saunters slowly through the fog. The figure silhouetted in the mist beneath the massive coaling plant is fellow trainspotter David Copus. Luckily for us we did not meet the depot foreman!

The second day of our Rail Rover trip was centred on the South Wales area. We visited six locomotive depots in the following order: Carmarthen, Goodwick, Whitland, Tondu, Abercynon and Radyr. This was a typical Radyr shed view, dominated by GWR tanks. Although this scene was captured eight years before our visit, I doubt whether the building or the classes of locomotives had differed much, except for the 'RR' class 0–6–2 tank No. 43 (fourth from left). Also in this view are Nos 8470, 4618, 5678, 7202, 7242 and 6607. *(Norman E. Preedy)*

Swansea East Dock Depot (87D). This 'Cardiff Railway' class 0–4–0 saddle-tank No. 1338, built in 1898, had almost reached the end of its working life with BR at the date of our visit in 1961. It was, however, taken into preservation at a later date and exists today in working order. *(The Leslie Hyde Collection)*

Machynlleth depot (89C). A Standard class '2' 2–6–0 locomotive No. 78000 quietly awaits its next duty. The stone water tower has long vanished from the scene but, surprisingly, the three-lane depot building is still intact today.

This 1961 photograph depicts '4073' (Castle) class 4–6–0 No. 7008 *Swansea Castle* entering Shrewsbury station. This locomotive carries an 81A (Old Oak Common) shed-plate. Note the magnificent signal gantry, partially visible, sadly removed in later years. The sign (top right) reads 'Water must not be discharged or spilled while standing at these signals'. Our visit to Shrewsbury was memorable not only for the signal gantry but also for the impressive LNWR signal box. *(The Leslie Hyde Collection)*

Gloucester (Barnwood) Depot (85C) was visited on day 7. This view shows the main depot building, including a rear view of the water tower. *(D.K. Jones Collection)*

Class '4300' 2–6–0 No. 7333 and Bulleid-designed 'West Country' class 4–6–2 No. 34002 *Salisbury* at Barnstaple, North Devon. The engine shed and water tower are partially visible in the distance. Both these types were 'on shed' during our visit, and of course a selection of 'M7' class 0–4–4 tanks, which included No. 30253 – thus giving me the pleasure of clearing all the SR steam locomotives by the summer of 1961. *(The Leslie Hyde Collection)*

Some of the author's 00 gauge model railway locomotives; the GW wagon is one of those superb card and plastic models that Tony Collett designed, as mentioned in chapter 20.

Class 'A1X', 0–6–0 tank locomotives were allocated to Fratton depot specifically to work the nearby Havant to Hayling Island branch. A 'Hayling Billy' tank could nearly always be found in Fratton yard along with numerous other classes whose numbers could be picked out from the station footbridge with the aid of binoculars. Here we see No. 32662 on the branch approaching North Hayling with some vintage carriages in the mid-1950s. *(Graham Scott)*

Is it Buddy Holly? No, and he never sounded anything like him either! The author with his acoustic guitar, purchased for £5 from Musical Homes in Fratton Road in 1960. The photograph was taken in the garden of 75 Penhale Road, Fratton.

My parents, George and Edith (Cis) Harvey on 20 June 1986 at the Farmhouse Hotel, Portsmouth. This was the happy occasion of their Golden Wedding anniversary. Sadly, both have now passed away, Dad in November 1987 and Mum in December 1998.

'Play Up Pompey' gummed labels leave their mark on this road sign at Wick in Caithness! Frank Allen is perched on top. Labels were also stuck on the reverse and the support of the sign.

Dunfermline depot (62C). This 1882-vintage 'Y9' class 0–4–0 saddle-tank No. 68101 has been put in a siding. Its rods have been removed, a sure sign that it is bound for the breaker's yard. July 1962. *(David Copus)*

Frank and David's final two visits on their 'Tartan Escapade' were south of the border, taking in the two Carlisle depots of Kingmoor (12A) and Upperby (12B). David took this picture of 'Royal Scot' class 4–6-0 No. 46107 *Argyll and Sutherland Highlander* at Kingmoor depot.

Above: Trevor Robson, the proud owner of a Ford Popular JAP 591, poses in a lay-by on the A3 outside Portsmouth in 1962.

Left: This is the Austin Seven car that Eddie Rooke bought for £5 in 1963. It is seen here at Horndean, near Portsmouth, with Eddie (top) and Trevor 'Haggis' Robson (showing off his hairy chest)! Note the checked caps, which were genuine Charlotte Street (local market) purchases. These were taken with us on nearly every trainspotting trip along with a plastic Pak-a-mac. Anoraks had not become popular at this date. What happy days!

Above: This is the Vale of Rheidol engine shed at Aberystwyth. The 'V of R' class 2–6–2 tank is No. 7 *Owain Glyndŵr*, named after the famous Welsh prince who rebelled against the English.

Right: This is Diane, the young lady from Bangor who gave us directions to the nearest doughnut shop! Note my cloth cap which she is proudly wearing.

Mold Junction depot (6B). Although this view of the yard was taken in 1960, the locomotives seen here were still 'in service', remarkably, during our visit on Tuesday 27 July 1965. From left to right: 'Jinty' 0–6–0 No. 47673 (6B), Standard class '5' 4–6–0 No. 73037, 'Black Five' 4–6–0 No. 45042 (6B) and Western Region class '6800' (Grange) 4–6–0 No. 6838 *Goodmoor Grange*. *(Allan Sommerfield Collection)*

Our farm camp site at Blackpool. The author, looking decidedly dejected, sporting cloth cap and sunglasses, poses in the rain. Note the deserted camp site – everyone, it seemed, had retreated to the luxury of their waterproofed tents! *(Eddie Rooke)*

The Blackpool illuminations are world famous, and this kind of scene, with a highly decorated tram travelling along the promenade, was but a dream for me and Eddie on this visit. Adverse weather conditions totally prevented us from leaving our tent and camping site. We received a thorough drenching, and the illuminations went unseen. *(The Leslie Hyde Collection)*

With about two months remaining before the demise of BR steam on the Southern Region, I captured this scene at Eastleight depot on 13 May 1967. Two Bulleid 'Pacifics', 'West Country' class Nos 34037 *Clovelly* (left) and 34040 *Crewkerne*, await their respective duties. Note that both engines have had their name-plates and crests removed. The future traction, in the shape of class '33' diesels, of which one is partially visible (far left), would be taking over some of the duties from these steam locomotives on Monday 10 July.

Stockport (Edgeley) depot (9B). Standing alone at the rear of the depot is withdrawn 'Black Five' 4–6–0 No. 45038. Note that its shed-code is painted on its smoke-box door and my piece of chalk came in handy to write '45038' for identification purposes.

Bolton depot (9K): an '8F' class 2–8–0 in immaculate condition. No. 48773 is about to go off shed and haul a special rail-tour. Note that the driver appears to be engrossed in reading a sheet of paper; perhaps it was his duties. On the right, looking rather filthy and neglected, is '5' class 4–6–0 No. 45394, its coupling rods removed and waiting its turn to be towed to the scrapyard.

Lostock Hall depot (10D). These are some of the lines of withdrawn steam locomotives that were awaiting their fate. They include '4' class 2–6–0s, '5' class 4–6–0s and '8F' class 2–8–0s. The large coaling plant dominates the skyline, while the depot building is on the right. It was one of the last three steam depots on BR.

Carnforth depot (10A). I took this general view looking towards the six-lane through straight shed. The steam locomotive on the left is '5' class 4–6–0 No. 45212, 'in steam' and awaiting its next duty.

Carnforth depot (10A). A pair of '9F' class 2–10–0 locomotives Nos 92004 and 92009 rest face-to-face on the scrap line. This picture probably sums up the sadness that I felt on this trip. Comparatively new steam locomotives were awaiting their doom because BR's 'modernisation plan' did not include steam.

we found in the amusement arcades then were very different from those of today. Pin-tables were very popular but usually the only thing to be won was a replay. To win money you had to play on primitive machines and try to get balls into designated holes, or you needed to play some of the earlier electronic machines which were linked to things like film stars or footballers. You had to bet on one of your choice, in the hope that the lights would stop flashing on the one you had chosen! Did I use the word 'primitive'? These machines were! The odds of getting a ball to drop into the correct hole were greatly increased if a friend pushed the glass top firmly into the machine. It didn't take us long to realise that the electronic film star machine worked on a predictable sequence of events which I seem to remember was just over thirty. This was duly written down, and for a few visits, we made a considerable profit. That was until one of the attendants spotted one of us referring to the list, and as a result banned us from that particular arcade!

We returned to Paddington station in plenty of time to board our overnight sleeper to South Wales. The locomotive hauling us was 'Castle' class 4–6–0 No. 5023 *Brecon Castle*.

Day 2: Paddington–Llanelli

We awoke from the comfort of our overnight sleeper train somewhere near Newport at around 6 a.m. The sleeping car attendant served us with complimentary tea and biscuits. Our arrival at Carmarthen station was at 7.05 a.m., where we were greeted by the shrill whistle of 'Hall' class 4–6–0 No. 6918 *Sandon Hall* as it travelled 'light' through the station. Here we began our engine shed visits. Carmarthen depot (87G) was the first visit and we saw twenty-five steam. From here we moved on to Goodwick depot (87J) where a mere nine steam were 'on shed'. The route to our next scheduled engine shed visit, Whitland, a sub-depot of Neyland (87H), was via Fishguard Harbour and Clarbeston Road stations. Whitland depot had just thirteen Western Region steam, all being tank designs; we noted that the shed building was constructed of corrugated-iron sheeting and was in a dismal, run-down state. Next on our busy timetable was the 12.41 p.m. to Bridgend, and much to our delight we were steam-hauled by 'Manor' class 4–6–0 No. 7825 *Lechlade Manor*; on our arrival we transferred to a modern diesel multiple-unit set bound for Tondu.

Tondu depot (88H) was visited and we saw thirty Western Region steam, all of which were tank designs. We returned to Bridgend on the 4.58 p.m. train to Cardiff General and on arrival, we caught a local train that took us through part of the Welsh Valleys to Abercynon. We arrived there at 6.25 p.m. and visited Abercynon depot (88E), where there were twenty steam 'on shed', once again all tank design types.

Our timetable had gone exactly to plan; by now evening was upon us and we were beginning to anticipate what would be our only night's sleep in a proper bed for the next seven days. But first we made our way from Abercynon to Radyr on the north-west outskirts of Cardiff and visited Radyr depot (88B), where we were surprised to note a '2800' class 2–8–0 No. 3804 amid a shed full of 0–6–2 side tanks and 0–6–0 pannier tanks, forty-three in all.

Our final journey of the day was the 9.15 p.m. 'Red Dragon' express between Cardiff General and Swansea, which had been hauled from Paddington by 'King' class 4-6-0 No. 6019 *King Henry V.* It must have been nearly 11 p.m. when we arrived at Swansea and walked briskly with Inky all the way to his relatives' house in Llanelli (which in those days was spelt Llanelly), looking forward to a well-earned night's sleep. Considering our lateness, we were given a very friendly welcome and fed with tea and bacon sandwiches, after which we told them about our hectic day. We then made our way to the upstairs bedroom and Eddie, the proud owner of a battery-operated transistor radio, tuned in to Radio Luxembourg, 208 on the dial in those days. We listened to the latest rock 'n' roll records until well past 12.30 a.m. – I shouldn't imagine Tony's relatives were too impressed with music being played at that hour! During the 1950s and early '60s this was the only radio station that was guaranteed to play the pop music of the time, with programmes sponsored by record companies that played all the new releases. The medium-wave reception was erratic to say the least, depending on where you were and the time of the evening.

There was only one double bed so we tossed a coin for who slept where. Inky got the floor, while Eddie slept with his feet at the head of the bed and I slept with my head on the pillow. It must have been near 1 a.m. before sleep overcame us. When waking at 5.30 the next morning the first things I saw were my mud-splattered Tuf shoes still firmly laced on my feet and several 'Play Up Pompey' gummed labels defacing the dressing-table mirror!

Day 3: Llanelli–Cardiff

After a very brief wash and tidy up we tucked into an appetising breakfast of sausage, egg, bacon and fried bread and thanked our Welsh friends for their kind hospitality. We checked our schedule for the day and headed off into the streets of Llanelli with our haversacks on our backs. There was a cold bite to the air and a deepening orange glow as the sun rose as we made our way to Llanelli engine shed. It was only 7 a.m., but we had all donned our sunglasses. On seeing a milk-float, we each bought a pint of milk which we drank as we walked. We must have looked a strange sight to any locals that morning, with our milk bottles, haversacks and sunglasses!

Llanelli depot (87F) was visited at about 7.40 a.m. and we found it crammed tight with Western Region steam, LMS '8F' class 2–8–0s, a selection of Standards, two WD 2–8–0s and one solitary '9F' class 2–10–0, No. 92210; in all, fifty-two steam were noted. We visited this depot without a permit and were fortunate not to meet the shed foreman at this early hour. After walking from the depot to Llanelli station we caught the 8.44 a.m. train to Swansea (High Street), enjoyably steam-hauled by 'Castle' class 4–6–0 No. 4094 *Dynevor Castle*, and arrived at 9.15 a.m. Our second engine shed visit of the day was then made Landore depot (87E). Here we saw a total of forty-one steam 'on shed', including 'Britannia' class 4–6–2s Nos 70025 *Western Star* and 70029 *Shooting Star*.

Completely out of character and probably to save us the expense of a taxi journey, we decided to 'hitch' a lift to the next depot on our schedule. This was Upper Bank, a former sub-depot of Swansea (Victoria), and a very small two-lane shed whose name came from its position perched high up on a narrow strip of land overlooking a wide river. We were lucky with our hitching and a friendly driver dropped us off near the depot. We saw just ten 0–6–0 pannier tanks at Upper Bank, but they filled the shed. From here we caught a United Welsh double-decker bus to Swansea, to visit Swansea East Dock depot (87D). At this shed we noted thirty-two Western Region steam and Standard class 5 4–6–0 No. 73094. A noteworthy diminutive 0–4–0 saddle-tank was No. 1338, built in 1898 for the Cardiff Railway. The *British Locomotive Shed Director* was of great assistance in locating the smaller and lesser-known engine sheds, although I had already visited engine sheds in the Cardiff and Swansea areas by this date. We three trainspotters were all good friends and always kept within sight of each other, especially as Eddie had the week's timetable in his possession, but this would change later in the week after differences of opinion.

We caught another bus to Duffryn Yard depot (87B), quite a substantial engine shed. Here we noted fifty Western Region steam and one '9F' class 2–10–0. Next in line were two depots at Neath. First was Neath (N & B) depot which produced ten 0–6–0 pannier tanks, and then Neath depot (87A) with thirty-five steam and just one 0–6–0 diesel shunter 'on shed'. The Neath & Brecon depot was, with Glyn Neath, a sub-depot of 87A and was close to the Tennant Canal. Our Sunday timetable was running smoothly so far and we were confident that we would finish the day at Cardiff General station waiting-room as planned.

Moving eastwards, we travelled from Swansea to Barry Island on the 5.24 p.m. diesel multiple-unit train, making sure to occupy the front seats behind the train driver to gain the maximum view of passing trains and lineside features. Our first visit in the Barry area was Barry scrapyard, owned by Dai Woodham. Though we could not have foreseen it, this scrapyard would in later years become an important railway graveyard; the location was successfully 'bunked' and we noted twenty Western Region steam locomotives being left to the ravages of time. Nearby was Barry depot (88C). Here we noted twenty-nine tank engines and '4300' class 2–6–0 No. 6365, which displayed a Gloucester (Horton Road) shed-plate. Next visited was Cardiff (Canton) depot (88A) and just like a top main-line shed should, it produced no fewer than ninety steam including a sighting of the last steam locomotive built for British Railways, '9F' class 2–10–0 No. 92220 *Evening Star*, along with six 'Britannias' and five 'Kings'.

It was late evening as we arrived at Newport; the station clock showed 8.50 and we still had three engine sheds to complete before the day's travels ended. First was Newport (Ebbw Junction) depot (86A), where we were rewarded with a large depot filled to capacity with a selection of Western Region classes and some very grimy-looking WD 2–8–0s – the 'on shed' total was 116. As on previous visits we left via the rear entrance and eventually found ourselves crossing a large allotment area via some narrow pathways to

Newport (Pill) depot (86B). We needed to be a bit wary here as we did not have a permit for our visit, but we need not have worried since as it was Sunday and no railwaymen were to be seen. Pill produced twenty-eight tank engines and eight 0–6–0 diesel shunters. From the dockland area of Newport was a thirty-minute walk. On the way to the city centre and the High Street station we bought bags of hot doughnuts, milk shakes and bars of chocolate from a small café and carried on walking while we eagerly consumed them. Eddie and I considered this our main meal of the day, which did not go down too well with Inky. He was obviously unimpressed by our idea of a reasonable meal, and it led to some friction between us. Nevertheless, we continued to follow our demanding timetable by catching a train to Severn Tunnel Junction.

Severn Tunnel Junction depot (86E) was our final visit. Entering the depot illegally via the end of the station platform and walking the length of the depot yard was definitely not the official route, but time was running out and this needed to be a swift visit. It was about 10 p.m., the light was fading and we were lucky, even though we had a permit, not to come into contact with the dreaded foreman. This depot produced fifty-seven steam, of which '4500' class 2–6–2 tank engine No. 4558 was resplendent in ex-works condition. Returning to the station via the same routes we successfully caught our scheduled train to Cardiff General, where we planned to get our aching heads down for some much-needed shuteye. We found ourselves sharing the main waiting-room and some very long hard wooden seats with several drunks and tramps also using the British Railways facilities as a dosshouse. It appeared that we would get very little sleep. We donned our cloth caps, covered ourselves with our plastic macs, rested our heads on our haversacks and tried desperately to get some sleep; it was nearly 1 a.m. before station staff entered the waiting-room. They promptly ordered the drunks and tramps to leave before they called the police. When they approached us and asked us politely why three teenagers were there at that time of night, we produced our valid Western Region Rail Rover tickets. Because we were waiting for our next scheduled train, the 4.45 a.m. to Treherbert, we were allowed to stay in the waiting-room, which by now was deserted. It was bliss to get our heads down knowing that there would be no unwelcome visitors. Even so, we were awake by 4 o'clock to stretch our legs, take a few swigs of fizzy drink and devour the remains of our chocolate bars from the previous night. Along with some crisps it was hardly an appetising breakfast but it kept us going for a few more hours!

Day 4: Cardiff–Hereford

Our departure for Treherbert was on time at 4.45 a.m. We travelled in a diesel multiple-unit via Radyr which gave us a further hour and forty-minute rest before another full day's programme of travelling and visiting. Treherbert depot (88F) was visited and here we noted ten tank engines, including '6100' class 2–6–2 tank No. 6108. We returned to Cardiff and departed from Queen Street station on another DMU bound for Caerphilly. On our arrival we could not help but notice the impressive castle, the largest in Britain, towering high above the town. Caerphilly Works was our next visit where we had our permit checked by the gateman and were introduced to a guide who would take us and other parties around. We noted a total of thirty-four Western Region steam 'in works' plus Standard class 4 4–6–0 No. 75001. An unexpected 'cop' for me was '6100' class 2–6–2 tank No. 6139 of Didcot, which 'cleared' this class of seventy tanks.

Returning again to Cardiff, we had sufficient time to spare to visit the Canton area and take some photographs. Initially we stood on the long footbridge which spanned the depot yard and noted some 'Hall' class 4–6–0s moving off shed; among those jotted down in my notes were Nos 5972 *Olton Hall*, 6909 *Frewin Hall* and 6943 *Farnley Hall*. Our day continued with a DMU train ride to Merthyr, where for the first time during our travels we were greeted with an exceptionally heavy downpour of rain. As trainspotters we were naturally ready for any such emergency and immediately put on our plastic macs, cloth caps and sunglasses, slung our haversacks over our shoulders and entered Merthyr depot (88D). We had no permit for this depot and when the foreman approached us a quick plan of action was called for. 'Leave it to me,' said Eddie. He then assumed a French accent – which he had learnt at school – and with a bit of arm-waving and some imitated accents from Inky and myself, the foreman assumed we were foreigners and could not converse, so we were allowed entry! There were fifteen steam 'on shed' – all tanks.

The rain having eased, we walked to Quakers Yard (Low Level) station, where we learnt that our 1.58 p.m. departure for Aberdare was due to depart from the High Level platforms. The High

Level station was deserted except for a lone elderly railwayman happily sweeping the opposite platform. We needed to ascertain which platform our train would depart from. Calling across to the railwayman, I asked, 'Is the 1.58 to Aberdare from this platform?' The railwayman stopped sweeping the platform and slowly turned towards us; in a deafening one-word answer, he replied 'Yes!' We were then steam-hauled to Aberdare by '5600' class 0–6–0 tank No. 6628. Aberdare depot (88J) was visited and produced thirty-four Western Region locomotives of various tank designs and, looking rather out of place, solitary '2800' class 2–8–0 No. 2886, shedded at Aberdare.

Our journey between Aberdare and Aberbeeg was steam-hauled by '5100' class 2–6–2 tank locomotive No. 4146. Aberbeeg depot (86F) had just eighteen tanks 'on shed', most of them panniers, of which one, No. 8417, had been withdrawn from service. Having done our planning carefully, at this point we changed our means of transport from train to bus and made our way to Pontypool via Crumlin, on the A467 and A462. Pontypool Road depot (86G) was well worth the bus ride as it produced 'on shed' sixty steam of many classes, ranging from pannier tanks to 'Hall' and 'Grange' 4–6–0s and LMS '8F' class 2–8–0 No. 48320 that carried a 2B shed-plate, Nuneaton. During our extensive travels in the Welsh Valleys we had noted at locations such as collieries, gas works and other industrial sites numerous privately owned working and non-working standard gauge saddle-tanks and side tanks. When BR steam ceased, these privately owned locomotives in their various environments continued to work, and when the collieries and other installations closed down many of the locomotives were purchased by preservation societies all over Great Britain.

Next on our list was Hereford depot (85C), where a mixture of Western, London Midland and Standards were 'on shed', and of note were 'Jubilee' class 4–6–0 No. 45726 *Vindictive* and two Standards, Nos 73090 and 78004; of the twenty-six locomotives, twenty-two were Western Region. By now we were in need of a square meal and we spotted a fish and chip shop soon after leaving the depot. Here we bought cod and chips, and ate them as we walked towards the station. We had also bought bottles of fizzy and a supply of crisps for later. We had our 'afters' sitting quietly on a wooden platform seat at Hereford station, stuffing ourselves silly with bars of chocolate from the station vending machines washed down with gulps of fizzy! At this time not only was Coca-Cola nothing like as popular as it is today, but drinks were sold in heavy glass bottles with screw tops, the empty bottle being returnable with a small deposit refunded.

Having some time to reflect on another day of intense travel, in which we visited six depots and one workshop, we checked our schedules for the remainder of the week. Our timetable now gave us some respite, as our next departure was shortly before midnight, bound for Shrewsbury.

Day 5: Hereford–Birmingham

Our overnight train from Hereford to Shrewsbury was very well patronised and as a result we found it difficult to find spaces for the three of us together. We eventually came across an empty compartment and had thoughts of a warm and uninterrupted night's sleep, but the first problem was that there was no steam heating and secondly other passengers found our compartment and tried to make conversation with us! The train took a considerable time to get to Shrewsbury, since it doubled as a newspaper and mail train and made many picking-up and off-loading stops. Our first priority at Shrewsbury was a hot drink but unfortunately the buffet was not open, so we had to buy cartons of cold milk from the station vending machines. At 7.30 a.m. we boarded a train bound for Chester General. A thirty-minute wait at this station provided us trainspotters with no fewer than twenty steam locomotives. Most of these were LMS types, though two Western Region locomotives were also noted: 'County' class 4–6–0 No. 1013 *County of Dorset* employed on a passenger train, and '4300' class 2–6–0 No. 5399 on a freight train.

Having recovered somewhat from our overnight journey, engaged in some exciting trainspotting and refreshed ourselves with ice-cold milk, we were now off to Wrexham, steam-hauled much to our delight by 'Hall' class 4–6–0 No. 4949 *Packwood Hall*. Our train arrived on time, as did nearly every train that we travelled on. We had British Railways to thank for enabling us to follow our carefully planned timetable with such precision. From Wrexham station we walked to Croes Newydd depot (89B), where nineteen steam were 'on shed'; of special interest was a 'J39' class 0–6–0 freight locomotive from the Eastern Region, No. 64930, which carried a

9G shed-plate, Gorton. Our next visit took us to Wellington (Salop) depot (84H), a three-lane depot where we noted just a dozen steam, including '2P' class 0–4–4 tank No. 41900.

Leaving the depot via Victoria Road we made the five-minute walk to the station, from where the next departure on our schedule would take us on quite a lengthy journey to Aberystwyth via Wolverhampton (Low Level), Shrewsbury, Welshpool, Moat Lane and Machynlleth. Aberystwyth depot at this date was a sub-depot of Machynlleth. Here we saw twelve steam 'on shed', of which seven were 'Manor' class 4–6–0s. The only narrow gauge steam railway operated by British Railways was our next visit. We did not travel on the train to Devil's Bridge but did 'bunk' the small Aberystwyth (Vale of Rheidol) depot where all three locomotives used on this scenic railway were noted. On return to the station, we caught a train to Machynlleth and once again were steam-hauled, this time by 'Manor' class 4–6–0 No. 7815 *Fritwell Manor*. The station clock told us that our arrival was at exactly 6 p.m. and the journey had been most enjoyable in the early evening sunshine, with a glorious backdrop of hills and the wide River Dovey never very far away. Travelling via Dovey Junction station, we wondered how passengers found their way to this location as it was set amid the salt marshes of the River Dovey. We then found out from a local passenger that the station was built solely for railway passenger exchanges and had *no* road access!

Machynlleth depot (89C) was a three-lane shed with a very friendly foreman (we did not encounter too many of these on our journeys). We spoke with him about the steam engines allocated to his depot and he told us that the 'Manor' class were his favourite, being so easy to handle; but he ended on a rather sad note, saying that in a year or so's time they would all be retired and sent to the scrapyard in favour of the diesel. This depot included nineteen steam, Standards Nos 75026, 78002, 78005, 78006, 82000, 82006 and 82036. Our timetable then took us to Oswestry on a DMU train which arrived at 9.10 p.m. Much to the delight of our companion Inky we found time to visit a small café near the station for sausage, fried egg, bacon and chips washed down with several cups of tea, an unplanned luxury that certainly revived our flagging enthusiasm.

Feeling totally revitalised, we then entered Oswestry depot (89D) and saw thirty steam 'on shed', twenty-one Western and nine LMS class 2 2–6–0s. Our next visit had to be treated rather cautiously as we had no permit to visit Oswestry Works. Our first task was to cross a deserted main-line track without being spotted by a nearby signalman. We achieved this successfully, but with the late evening light fading rapidly we came face-to-face with a railway worker as we approached the main building. We half expected him to tell us to bugger off but much to our relief he asked us instead if we were intending to visit the works. 'Hurry up as I am about to lock up!' he said when we told him. We thanked him gratefully, quickly visited the works and noted six steam. These included Nos 822 *The Earl* and 823 *The Countess*, 0–6–0 tanks designed for the Welshpool & Llanfair Railway on a 2ft 6in gauge; the noting of '9000' class ('Dukedog') 4–4–0 No. 9017 was a surprise – and in later years it would be preserved on the Bluebell Railway in Sussex.

This visit marked the end of another action-packed day. Apart from the heavy downpour at Merthyr the previous day the weather had been sunny. For us trainspotting freaks it was time again for the thrill and adventure of overnight train travel. Our schedule took us on a late-night train from Oswestry to Birmingham (New Street), affording us ample time for some shut-eye. Before we all settled down, however, we found separate toilets and availed ourselves of the luxury of hot water and soap as we had by now developed an odour problem! If you have ever thought about trying to wash your complete body in the toilet compartment of a speeding train especially with a full basin of hot water slurping about I suggest you reconsider. Nevertheless, we did manage some form of decent wash, and passengers travelling in our carriage must have wondered what we were up to when we returned sporting clean faces with our hair wet and neatly combed! The problem of smelly socks was alleviated firstly by washing them in the handbasin of the toilet and secondly by dangling them out of the carriage window to dry them, much to the annoyance of other passengers! A change of clothing was out of the question – we took none! At one point a shirt was dangled out of a speeding train window to 'give it some air'!

Day 6: Birmingham–Worcester

Our overnight train from Oswestry only gave us snatches of sleep. When the train jolted to a halt I peeped out of the misted carriage window and saw the station clock at Birmingham (New Street) showing 2.15 a.m. We were all in need of some proper sleep, and hoped to achieve this in the large waiting-room. To our surprise we found the waiting-room almost full of people. Were they waiting for trains or just using the facilities for somewhere to sleep? We thought that maybe some of them may have been trainspotters pursuing their harmless hobby just like us. Station staff must have moved on any tramps or drunks, as there were no sightings of them. By 3.30 a.m. the waiting-room was still crowded and too noisy to allow any form of sleep, so we opted to walk the streets to ease our aching legs and get some fresh air. There was a cold chill and the sky was dark grey. After walking for nearly an hour, the only signs of activity were Birmingham City Corporation men watering the street gutters.

Partially revitalised, we returned to New Street station to begin another day on the rails, departing for Shrewsbury on the 4.40 a.m. train, where we had better luck and found an empty compartment with the heating switched on. It did not take us long before sleep overcame us, but in all honesty we really needed more.

But by 7.50 a.m. we were making the day's first visit, Shrewsbury depot (89A), where we saw forty-eight steam 'on shed'. These included Western, LMS and Standards, of which the latter comprised Nos 73025, 73034, 73092 and 73096, the last mentioned being preserved and resident on the Mid-Hants Railway today. The very tall LNWR signal-box bathed in early morning sunshine just outside the station was an impressive sight. We travelled next to the West Midlands to take in the three Wolverhampton depots and Stafford Road Works. First came Wolverhampton (Stafford Road) depot (84A), where we noted twenty-five steam, then Oxley depot (84B), where we noted twenty-eight steam and six 0–6–0 diesel shunters. The third depot was Bushbury depot (21C), where we only saw nine LMS steam 'on shed', including '2F' class 0–6–0 No. 58124. As we had no permit to visit Stafford Road Works we entered the yard via the back entrance through a small gate in Gorsebrooke Road, then we split up and completed our visit without any hitches. We noted thirty-five steam and one solitary 0–6–0 diesel shunter, and I took a photograph of Inky standing on the frames of Standard class 5 4–6–0 No. 73037 in the works yard.

A visit to the local bakery provided bags of hot jam doughnuts covered in sugar that were a welcome relief for our empty stomachs. Once again Inky wanted to visit a café for a more substantial meal but with a very tight schedule before us there was no time for such luxuries. Tyseley depot (84E) was our next visit and here we saw forty steam and three diesel shunters. One of the steam, '5100' class 2–6–2 tank No. 5192, was 'stored' with a 'NOT TO BE MOVED' sign on its buffer beam. We then made our way to Stourbridge Junction depot (84F) where we found a very busy scene: thirty-four steam locomotives were noted and half a dozen diesel shunters. Our next visit was Kidderminster depot (84G), where a selection of Western Region classes was noted. Here we saw three diesel rail-cars, No W21, W25 and W31.

Following our visit to Kidderminster we caught a train to Worcester. The early evening sun was beginning to set as we made our way on a three-car DMU train through some truly delightful English countryside with apple orchards abounding on either side of the railway and lush green fields and meandering rivers never very far away. Unfortunately a bit of a fracas broke out between Inky and me on this train which saw raised fists, but, restrained by Eddie, our difference of opinion regarding the lack of decent meals during the week eventually cooled down before any passengers complained. Our tempers were a little frayed to say the least, but nevertheless we continued together to Worcester.

It was a five-minute walk from Shrub Hill station to Worcester depot (85A), where we noted thirty Western Region steam and, among other types, 'Britannia' class 4–6–2 No. 70020 *Mercury*. We did not attempt to visit Worcester Works, sited on the opposite side of the main line to the depot, but we did note 'Castle' class 4–6–0 No. 7005 *Lamphey Castle* and 'Manor' class 4–6–0 No. 7819 *Hinton Manor* along with a few others awaiting attention in the works yard. In the late evening following a day of glorious sunshine and blue skies, we found some time for relaxation in the waiting-room of Shrub Hill station. After the day's punishing timetable all three of us were exhausted and sleep would have been inevitable if we had laid ourselves out on those long hard wooden seats and closed our eyes to the outside world – but we still had a train to catch. The next stage of our travels was quite lengthy and involved an overnight train from Worcester to London followed by a quick turn-around and back to Gloucester the next morning. This was all part of our schedule, the plan being that the overnight train would enable us to get some proper sleep before completing our final few days of the Western Region Rail Rover.

It was here, following our fracas, that Inky decided to go it alone for the remainder of the week. Eddie gave him all the final details of the timetable in case he wished to rejoin us later. With Inky now departed, the waiting-room at Shrub Hill became a café in which we consumed our main meal; as it was the end of May this meal consisted of a pound bag of cherries each! Eddie's craving for cherries not only at this location but throughout the week also led me to become hooked on cherries, and countless half-pound bags were devoured whenever possible. Later that evening, before catching our overnight express to Paddington, we visited a nearby fish and chip shop and bought six pennyworth. After sharing a bottle of lemonade our needs were satisfied. We sat quietly on the station platform seat and underlined our 'cops' for the week so far in our *Ian Allan ABC Combined Volume*, and likewise in our *Loco Shed Book* – the latter at that date would have set us back just 2s 6d.

Day 7: Worcester–Taunton (via London)

The overnight train from Worcester was diesel-hauled, and for the very first time during the week we encountered a late arrival. We reached Paddington forty-five minutes late, but fortunately this did not upset our schedules as we had allowed seventy-five minutes at this terminus. In our half an hour we had a much needed clean-up, and still found time to look in at the station buffet and buy some sandwiches and jam doughnuts. Our departure for Bristol was at 9.15 a.m., and we were diesel-hauled. At Temple Meads we quickly changed trains and travelled to Gloucester. First visited was Gloucester (Horton Road) depot (85B), where we noted thirty-five steam and two diesels, before moving on to Gloucester (Barnwood) depot (85C) where LMS 0–6–0s were predominant, although several 'Jubilee' class 4–6–0s were also 'on shed', including Nos 45576 *Bombay* and 45668 *Madden*. Out of a total of twenty-nine steam, the most interesting to us was ancient Deeley Midland-designed '0F' class 0–4–0 tank No. 41535. Next visited was Lydney depot, this being a sub-depot of Horton Road. Only six 0–6–0 pannier tanks were noted at this location.

Following this visit, we had some time to spare and chanced to see a nearby public house. It was out of character for us but we went in and had a ploughman's lunch washed down with a half of lager and lime. We were probably quite guilty that Inky was not with us to enjoy what he would have classed as a decent meal. Drinking alcohol was virtually unheard of on our trainspotting trips. We certainly never took any with us, and all that I can recall is that during one of our mammoth visits to London depots we visited an off-licence adjacent to Cricklewood depot and bought a quart bottle of cider. Four of our group were unable to finish it off but we goaded our friend Stan from Hyde Park Road, Southsea, into consuming the remaining half – it certainly livened him up!

Fully refreshed, we caught a train from Lydney to Bristol, travelling via Severn Tunnel Junction, and then Temple Meads, under that famous Brunel masterpiece, the station roof, to Taunton via Highbridge and Bridgwater. Along our route we noted '2251' class 0–6–0 No. 2232, 'Jubilee' 4–6–0 No. 45606 *Falkland Islands* and Standard class 3 2–6–2 tank No. 82001.

It was almost midnight as we walked from Taunton station to the depot entrance. It had been a somewhat strange day without our companion, and we wondered with some concern whether he would be able to cope on his own. We hoped that he would show up during one of our visits – at least he had a copy of our timetable.

Oddly enough, my previous visit to Taunton depot had taken place in the small hours, during a Southern Region Rail Rover in 1960 with Bill Jenkins and Jim Lawrence. On that occasion it was at 2.40 a.m. and on this visit it was 12.15 a.m., and we had no permit! We successfully 'bunked' Taunton depot (83B), but even if we had had a permit I don't think the foreman would have been too impressed. Luckily, we did not meet a soul, and we witnessed the depot in a ghostly silence. We half expected to bump into a railwayman but with thirty steam noted we quietly departed and returned to the station.

Day 8: Taunton–Fratton

Our many engine shed visits during this week had occasionally led to the shed foreman checking our permit. It always brought a wry smile to the official's face when Eddie's permit folder was opened – the inside cover revealed a glossy colour picture of a nude woman staring him in the face! This no doubt helped to distract him from certain details on the permit (such as the date and the number in party) that we may have altered ourselves for obvious reasons! On this eight-day adventure we had official permits for most of our depot visits, but that's not to say that the remainder were not previously used sheets borrowed from David Copus, and suitably amended – with, of course, the nude picture accompanying them!

To complete our eight days on the rails, all that remained was for us to visit three more engine sheds, these being Laira (Plymouth), Penzance and St Blazey. We left Taunton at 3.10 a.m., diesel-hauled by 'Warship' class No. D835 *Pegasus* to Exeter (St David's). On our arrival we rested in the same waiting-room that I had used a year previously on a Southern Region Rail Rover. Our next departure was at 5.17 a.m., on the 1.10 a.m. train originating from Waterloo bound for Plymouth. Its arrival at North Road station was on time at 7.40 a.m., from where it was quite a demanding walk to Laira depot. First we refreshed ourselves with piping-hot tea from the station buffet and then, any remnants of tiredness now completely dispelled, went for a brisk 2-mile walk in the bright early morning sunshine.

At Laira (Plymouth) depot (83D) we noted twenty-five WR steam and nineteen main-line diesels, a sure sign that steam was on the decline. After the return walk to North Road station we enjoyed a further cup of tea at the buffet, and did not have to wait too long for our departure to Penzance. Some of the steam jotted down in our notebooks en route to Penzance were an 0–6–0 pannier tank No. 3702, Prairie tank No. 4566, and two 'Grange'

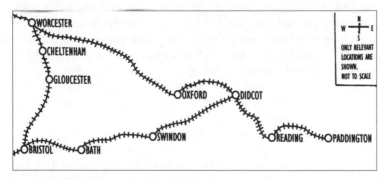

Rather than spend the night on Worcester station and then travel the short distance to Gloucester the next morning, we travelled on an overnight train to Paddington and caught the 9.15 a.m. to Bristol, where we changed trains and then travelled to Gloucester. Only trainspotters would attempt such a diverse route!

class 4–6–0s 6824 *Ashley Grange* and 6870 *Bodicote Grange*, the former with which I 'cleared' the class of eighty locomotives, and '9400' class 0–6–0 pannier tank No. 8466.

We could have caught a Western National double-decker bus from Penzance station to the depot but it was a sunny morning so we opted for the twenty-minute walk. We were rewarded by noting fourteen steam at Penzance depot (83G). These included eight 'Granges' and two 'County' 4–6–0s, Nos 1003 *County of Wilts* and 1004 *County of Somerset*. We walked back to the station and, having some time on our hands before the departure for St Blazey, visited the town and bought a few souvenirs such as sticks of rock and table mats. Naturally, before our return to the station we made the customary visit to a fish and chip shop. Both Eddie and I were relieved when looking for an empty compartment to be reunited with Inky. Our group of three stayed together for the remainder of our adventure, our differences now forgotten, and we happily shared our separate experiences since splitting up thirty-six hours earlier.

Our final visit, St Blazey (83E), was made and here we saw fourteen steam and four 0–6–0 diesel shunters 'on shed'. This building was of a semi-roundhouse type, only a few of which existed on British Railways; I had the pleasure of cabbing '1600' class 0–6–0 pannier tank, No. 1624, at this depot.

As we made our way by diesel-hauled train from St Blazey to London (Paddington) we felt a double twinge of both sadness and relief that our 'greatest adventure' was coming to an end. Thoughts crossed our minds of partaking in further trips, or of stretching our limits even further by participating in an All-line Rail Rover of Great Britain. Whatever our plans might have been for future trainspotting trips, we all came to the conclusion that our hectic, self-imposed eight days on the rails, despite some personal differences, had been thoroughly enjoyable, an experience that we would always remember.

Just for the record, my scribbled notes in my spotter's book reveal that I took the sum of just £4 spending money with me; from this I needed to retain 18s for my tube train across London and a single ticket from Waterloo to Fratton. When I reached home safely my mum was much relieved, and it was utter bliss to remove my Tuf shoes, sip a hot cup of tea and tuck into a slice of mum's home-made apple pie!

17

Plain Stupid, but Good Fun!

The early 1960s saw us teenagers meeting more regularly not only on the station footbridge but also at Pompey's home games, live music events, the youth club and at football training (for Sunday League matches). The last mentioned would take place at Kingston Recreation Ground in St Mary's Road, Bransbury Park, Milton, or in the summer months on the grass area adjoining Canoe Lake, almost next to Southsea seafront. During evening sessions after sunset the promenade lights would provide us with some floodlighting! We got around by walking or bus, although Eddie Rooke became at about this time the proud owner of a Lambretta scooter and later a succession of cars – but these were rarely used to get us around within Portsea Island. In addition to all these pastimes, we also found time to engage in some rather unorthodox and stupid activities.

Frank Allen claimed to have invented the 'Sponical'. This was a high-pitched noise caused by speaking the word 'Sponical' while holding the nose tightly with one hand and repeatedly moving the other hand on and off the throat at the same time. It was not long before many of my trainspotting friends produced their own versions. These could be heard at Fratton Park supplementing the Pompey gong, during our railway trips and at the youth club, among other places. The word 'Sponical' originally derived from 'Fred Spon' of *Goon Show* fame.

Following a Sunday excursion or a football excursion from Portsmouth, British Railways permanent-way workers checking the tracks would have been most puzzled to discover a complete white toilet roll unwound and laid between the tracks. Needless to say, this was something to do with us! It was a precision operation and took two of us to complete. Standing in the toilet of the last carriage of the train, one of us would hold the toilet roll (a finger in each end) over the lavatory pan while the other would flush the toilet, first making sure that the complete operation was being carried out on a suitably curved section of track. The discharge of water would unravel the roll, with the outcome that we could look out of the carriage window and see the thin white line of a fully unwound toilet roll between the railway lines!

When we travelled on Sunday excursions from Portsmouth Harbour station we invariably secured a complete compartment or sometimes two next to each other; in those days we did not bother with advance seat reservations, we just made sure our party was first on the train! We would have visited a newsagents beforehand and bought a packet of round balloons. As soon as we found an empty compartment a balloon was blown up and a game of head tennis would commence.

There was always a small white plastic warning sign with black lettering to be observed above the railway carriage doors. It read 'Do not lean out of the window', and was displayed for obvious reasons. I often wonder what would have happened had any of us trainspotters sustained a serious injury through ignoring this warning, which we did repeatedly in order to obtain the numbers of passing locomotives. Not only did it fail to prevent us from tempting fate but on many of our trips the sign would be amended with a black marker to read 'Do not clean soot off the window' – very appropriate in those days when steam trains left their mark on train windows.

What with our telephone directory names, our silly songs, our sponicals, bog rolls, the gong and the Pompey gummed labels, I have come to the conclusion that we were a very easily pleased bunch of teenagers in those days. One thing is certain – we were never violent, and muggings were unheard of. Obviously trains were our number one hobby but I do wonder whether any of

| DO NOT LEAN OUT OF THE WINDOW |
| DO NOT CLEAN SOOT OFF THE WINDOW |

The top plastic sign displayed above the carriage doors was slightly amended!

our silly antics ever actually offended anyone. We might have an occasional complaint about noise when a head tennis game was in progress but generally we were a happy-go-lucky group of lads and I can't remember us ever being called a gang. To me this would have meant that we rushed around on unruly rampages. This was not the case, but having said that I do recall that we made our own fireworks leading up to Guy Fawkes night and dispatched them outside the homes of some of our close friends!

David Copus and his pals always made a great thing of the fireworks season. All sorts of fireworks – bangers, rockets and jumping jacks, to name but a few – were bought, and the active contents were removed and mixed. An early attempt, mixed in a small paint tin, resulted in a very black mark on David's bedroom ceiling and incurred his father's wrath! Undeterred, David continued with further experiments. One night a coffee tin crammed tight with the contents of numerous fireworks was deposited in a quiet alley just off Albert Road, Southsea. The extra long paper was lit and everyone retired to a safe distance. Then from out of nowhere, an elderly lady appeared, heading straight for the firework. We shouted at her in an attempt to stop her but it was too late – the firework went off! The resulting explosion was negligible, but the light effect was stunning, transforming a dark night into near daylight!

There was great rivalry between the local grammar schools (most of my friends attended the Southern Grammar), and in the fireworks season it was commonplace for bicycle handlebars to be used as launching pads to fire rockets at boys from the Portsmouth and Northern Grammar schools. Another use for handlebars was to blow into them, and use them as a musical backing for the Pompey gong when supporting Portsmouth FC at Fratton Park!

18

Two in a Tent

A summer weekend in July 1961 was the occasion for Eddie Rooke and me to try our hand at camping. This proved to be an exceptionally memorable experience. At this date Eddie owned a blue Lambretta scooter, registration number WTP 977, on which we had often travelled locally to visit the depot at Eastleigh (71A). Saturday 22 and Sunday 23 July will always remain in my memory – Eddie and his Lambretta were going to tour south-west England, and I would be the pillion passenger.

Before the weekend we had jointly purchased a small tent and decided to 'blood' it on this special trainspotting weekend, undertaken principally in hope of noting my last Southern Railway steam locomotive, 'M7' class 0–4–4 tank No. 30253, allocated then to the north Devon town of Barnstaple. We began our journey in lovely sunshine from Eddie's house in Fratton early on Saturday afternoon and were looking forward to a 'new adventure'. We had put a lot of thought into our route, which included engine sheds to be 'bunked' at twelve different locations. Unfortunately, we did not do likewise with our camping plans.

We travelled the A27 via Fareham and Southampton and then through the New Forest to make our first visit to the depot at Bournemouth (71B). While here we also visited the Central and West stations; all in all we saw thirty-two steam locomotives, of which eight were class 'M7' 0–4–4 tanks. Moving on to the depot at Weymouth (71G), we noted thirty-five steam; of interest here were three class '1366' 0–6–0 pannier tanks Nos 1367, 1368 and 1369. The next stop was the small one-lane engine shed at Bridport, at that date a sub-depot of Weymouth, where we found the building empty. Travelling along the A35 coast road via Charmouth and Sidmouth

we eventually arrived at Exeter, where we first visited Exmouth
Junction depot (72A) and were rewarded by noting fifty-two steam
'on shed', but not before we had to play 'hide-and-seek' from the
shed foreman! Of note were five class 'Z' heavy 0–8–0 tank engines,
Nos 30950, 30952, 30953, 30955 and 30957. Having travelled
the short distance through Exeter we visited the Western Region
depot, Exeter (83C), noting just twenty-six steam and two main-
line 'Warship' class diesels. This was followed by a quick visit to the
Central station, where we saw a hive of activity, including two more
'Z' 0–8–0s, Nos 30951 and 30956, Standard class 2 2–6–2 tank No.
84021, and two Bulleid Pacifics both employed on passenger trains
to and from Waterloo, Nos 34033 *Chard* and 34098 *Templecombe*.

It was nearing 9 p.m. and we had not eaten since we had left
Portsmouth. Very conveniently we located a fish and chip shop in
central Exeter where we both revived ourselves with large portions
of the usual, and then the familiar 'afters' of a large glass bottle of
lemonade. On this trip on which I took my usual trainspotter's
haversack, I had included some smelly egg sandwiches and a slice
of my mum's apple pie, but after our chip shop visit I decided to
reserve them for the next morning's breakfast. Suitably revived,
we took the A377 road to Barnstaple, but on reaching Crediton
the light was beginning to fade fast and it was then that we both
decided to look for a suitable field in which we could pitch our
tent. Although Eddie had some basic experience with the Scouts
some years previously, neither of us really had any idea what to
expect in this new venture. We found and entered what looked like
a suitable grassy field beside the main road, ideally sheltered by a
hedge: it appeared to be the perfect spot in which to pitch our tent.
Being a new toy for us, the tent was not erected until after about
half an hour of frigging about and a few swear words! Darkness
was setting in rapidly and we both retired to the luxury of our new
accommodation. We kept ourselves warm by putting on our plastic
macs and wearing our cloth caps, and made ourselves reasonably
comfortable. Supper came in the form of a packet of Smith's crisps
and a swig of fizzy drink as we listened to Radio Luxembourg on
Eddie's transistor radio. Pure bliss, we thought, and sleep overcame
us soon after I had set the alarm clock for 7.30 a.m.

Something must have woken me at 12.30 a.m. – I glanced at
my watch and forgetting I was in a small tent immediately stood

upright, bringing the tent to the ground around us. Eddie woke up and let loose a few choice words, but our second attempt at erecting the tent was much easier and quicker than our initial attempt! We settled down once again but I need not have bothered with the 7.30 alarm – we experienced a second rude awakening at 5.30 a.m. with the sound of cattle hooves. Peering out of the tent we realised our ideal camping site was actually a farmer's field: the sight of a herd of cows, or maybe bulls, put a scare into us and all we wanted to do was to get out of that field! Our departure was extremely hurried: we literally pulled the tent down and rolled it into a ball, jumped onto the scooter and left the field in the nick of time, just as a farmer brandishing a shotgun was rapidly approaching. All this excitement and it was still only 5.30 on Sunday morning! Our first attempt at camping was memorable, to say the least.

Having made a somewhat earlier start than anticipated, we now had some hours to spare; after travelling a few miles along the road towards Barnstaple away from the offending field, we stopped at a lay-by where breakfast was for me those smelly boiled-egg sandwiches and a slice of apple pie, rather flattened after our camping escapade. We stopped a passing milk-float and bought bottles of milk that we drank while in the lay-by. Following breakfast, we re-packed the tent and secured it safely to the scooter before setting out again for Barnstaple at around 6.30 a.m. We reached Barnstaple depot (72E) at 7 a.m. and the dull, misty conditions appeared to offer few photographic opportunities. Nevertheless I did manage half a dozen views, and much to my delight was rewarded with the sight of my final SR steam locomotive, No. 30253, at the entrance to the depot. At this wooden depot, which looked as if it had seen better days, we saw an array of steam classes which totalled nineteen in all, including two WR Moguls Nos 7304 and 7305, three Bulleid Pacifics Nos 34065 *Hurricane*, 34076 *41 Squadron* and 34081 *92 Squadron,* and some Ivatt-designed 2–6–2 tanks, including Nos 41298 and 41312.

With our mission to note No. 30253 successfully completed, we continued on our next stage to Taunton. En route we came across a railway station with the name Portsmouth Arms where we were fortunate to note 'N' class 2–6–0 No. 31840. The 'bunking' of Taunton depot (83B) was virtually completed when the dreaded foreman suddenly appeared from nowhere and demanded to see our permit. We were ordered to leave but we had already noted thirty-one steam locomotives. Moving on to Yeovil depot (72C), we saw eighteen steam 'on shed', including Fratton-allocated class 'U' 2–6–0 No. 31637. Leaving the depot we looked briefly into Pen Mill station and then continued our journey to Templecombe depot (82G). At this depot we noted eighteen steam, which included WR, LMS and Standards. The next visit was the small sub-depot of Westbury, Frome, where we saw four pannier tanks crammed into the one-lane a timber-built shed. Our final engine shed visit of the weekend was to be Westbury depot (82D). This was successfully 'bunked', and we noted thirty-five steam 'on shed', with classes ranging from GWR pannier tanks to 2–6–2 side tanks, 'Hall' 4–6–0s, 'Grange' 4–6–0's, '4300' 2–6–0s, LMS class '8F' 2–8–0 No. 48459 and solitary 'Castle' class 4–6–0 No. 5092 *Tresco Abbey* – quite a selection.

It was approaching early evening on the Sunday as we followed the A36 road homeward via Salisbury towards Southampton and Portsmouth. Although not officially included in our visits, we decided upon arrival in Portsmouth to 'bunk' Fratton depot (70F) to see if any Western Region steam locomotives were 'on shed'. We were lucky to note one 'Hall' class 4–6–0 that had brought in an excursion to Portsmouth Harbour. The dreaded 'Old B' of a foreman suddenly appeared from nowhere, and decided, even on a Sunday evening, to give us a ticking off. Anyway, we had already noted fourteen steam and three 0 6 0 diesel shunters and taken a photograph of a class 'A1X'!

On checking our mileage, we saw that we had completed a total of 420 miles. It was agreed I should pay Eddie the sum of 10s towards petrol costs. This trip was the fore-runner of many more that included taking our jointly owned tent. As the years progressed we learnt the acquisition of a sleeping-bag was to our advantage, but we never did learn that to have water-proofed the tent would have saved us from numerous drenchings!

19

Pranks and Protection

Although we travelled on our day trips, Sunday excursions, football excursions and other trains as a happy bunch of teenagers basically seeking adventure and the thrill of live steam, many of our group, myself included, had a somewhat mean streak in our actions towards our travelling companions. These actions were never intended to cause harm or danger, but for those who instigated the prank it was a great source of amusement.

On long trips, especially on a return journey when some of us had dozed off, it was common practice to transfer someone's satchel or haversack to the luggage rack above their heads; on arrival back at Fratton he would be frantically searching the seats and the floor. We made sure that the carriage door remained open until the relieved companion left clutching his bag! Hiding a friend's trainspotting notebook was another antic which gave us cause for amusement, that is until the person picked on was you! Whenever we took the Pompey gong on away football excursions we inevitably removed it from its carrier bag near the end of our homeward journey and gave it a few hefty bashes to awaken any sleepers among our party. To see the look on their faces was highly amusing!

Another prank would cause much confusion to sleeping members of our group when returning home on a Sunday excursion and nearing Portsmouth in the early hours of Monday morning. While three or four in our compartment were dozing soundly, the remainder of us, wide awake, would quietly gather up our belongings and transfer to the next compartment. On awaking and finding us gone, our friends' first confused thoughts would be that we had already alighted from the train and they had ended their trip at either Portsmouth Harbour station or Fratton carriage sidings! This prank certainly worked on me!

One excursion to Cardiff was so amusing for our travelling companions that it almost caused the young victim to make it his first and last trainspotting trip. The youngster we picked on had dozed off on approaching the General station and certain of the others carefully tied his shoelaces together. On arrival at Cardiff, we needed to alight quickly from the train to catch a connection to Barry Island but the young lad, on trying to stand up, crumpled to the floor of the carriage. From someone of his tender age the vocabulary of obscenities was quite astonishing. When he realised what had happened he rapidly undid the laces and since we did not want him to miss the connecting train we stood at the carriage door and kept it open. This irritated the train guard as he was waiting to give the train the 'right away'.

Another source of amusement for us trainspotters on group trips was to produce a rather rude sound achieved by putting your hand under your armpit and squeezing. It proved to be an embarrassment for nearby passengers and we got some strange looks! Other outlets for this flatulent obscenity included the youth club, the beach and the changing-room when playing in a Sunday League football match.

On one of our trainspotting trips, travelling between Reading and Swindon, one of our group, eager to answer the call of nature, found that every single toilet on the train appeared to be permanently engaged, and mini-queues of desperate ladies had formed, all waiting to spend a penny. On further investigation, we discovered that another older group of trainspotters was responsible. Armed with a ball of string and a pair of scissors, they had visited each toilet, shut the door, pulled the string (thereby locking the door from inside) – and then cut the string, ensuring that entry was impossible. There were numerous distressed ladies on the train on that day! For people waiting for trains at Swindon, it must have been a strange sight to see a mass exodus of passengers from our train heading directly to the station toilets!

Some of the pranks I have described in this chapter may seem hard to believe, but we trainspotters had been involved in setting them up over a period of years. The results were often viewed with a wry smile, and perhaps a touch of guilt. One such prank on the return journey of a trip to London organised by the Portsmouth Southern Grammar School Railway Club, will remain forever etched in my mind. One of our party had obtained a copy of the notorious *Health and Efficiency*. In the late 1950s this was just about the only obtainable magazine that displayed the naked attributes of the female body. The 'Page 3' topless beauties that we know so well today were many years away from introduction.

On this particular night the electric-unit train back to Portsmouth was very sparsely occupied. The opportunity was seized to unscrew all the advertising pictures from behind their glass frames in two adjacent compartments. The removed pictures were carefully deposited in the string luggage racks and selected pages from *Health and Efficiency* were placed in the frames! I dread to think how the carriage cleaners at Fratton reacted when they discovered such an extensive display of naked women!

Protected from Above

Whenever I pursued my beloved hobby of trainspotting, whether in the company of others or alone as in my later years, I always knew there were possible risks involved. Would I be robbed of my money and railway ticket, or attacked by a gang of yobbos or maybe have a fall and break an arm? Visions of such incidents entered my mind before setting out on a trip and yet, like my fellow companions, I was oblivious to any danger that might be lurking just around the corner. In the early days of my railway travels my parents did not have the luxury of a telephone, so if anything dreadful had happened to me the first they would have known about it would have been when a policeman came knocking on their door.

Although I never admitted it, even to my closest pals, I honestly felt that I was in some way being blessed by angels from above and that there really was a God watching over me, protecting me on my every adventure. This feeling probably stemmed from my religious involvement in my early teens when my mum and dad insisted that I attend Sunday morning church services at St Winifred's Church in George Street, railway trips permitting! This Sunday school began while I resided in Fifth Street and even after my parents had moved house to Penhale Road, about a mile and a half away, my attendance continued for quite a considerable time. Did I attend church to confess my trespasses on British Railways property and the illegal 'bunking' of locomotive depots? I don't think so, but I must admit I did feel a tinge of guilt whenever I knelt down to recite the Lord's Prayer.

My parents instilled a certain degree of discipline into my way of life, both as an only child and also in my hobby of trainspotting. Consequently I learned that I could not always have everything my own way. Sometimes this resulted in some proposed railway visits being forbidden for one reason or another. Listening later to my companions' stories about trips that I had missed out on was hard to stomach.

Whether or not I was being protected from above, I never had the slightest doubt when embarking on a trainspotting adventure that I had nothing to fear in the big outside world. The safety of British Railways travel was taken for granted. Even before the days of overcrowded roads, trains were always the number one mode of transport for me and most of my pals. As long as I was with others, walking through seedy backstreets, alleyways and areas of ill repute in search of grim, smoke-filled engine sheds, especially in the London area, was never a problem either during the day or at night. In fact, we were simply unaware that there might be danger lurking nearby, something that modern trainspotters have to be constantly alert for, with muggings and assaults an everyday occurrence.

Perhaps the beginnings of my religious belief date back to 1947, when I was only six years old. I vividly remember being admitted to the Royal Hospital, Commercial Road, Portsmouth, suffering from double pneumonia. My life was in the balance. I recall a nurse peering down at me as I was lying in the hospital bed, and her comforting words: 'You're going to be all right, Michael.' I must have in some way consciously thanked God for my recovery. Whenever I attended Sunday school in later years, these words would be in my thoughts.

20

An Abundance of Pastimes

Trainspotting and the railway scene were far from being the only activities of our leisure time, and numerous other indulgences kept us fully occupied.

Nearly every station of note on British Railways had in its vicinity a hotel or public house connected to the railway. Fratton station was no exception, and had the Railway Hotel, on the corner of Claremont and Walmer roads, two minutes' walk from the station. For us teenagers, growing up in the rock and roll era of the 1960s, the hotel was our nearest live music venue. It was here every Thursday evening in the early 1960s that we were entertained with that infectious sound known as rhythm and blues – and there were no admission costs!

The lead singer was a clean-cut young man called Paul Jones and the band Manfred Mann. Paul was a local lad and the band performed in a small function room in the Claremont Road side of the building. As the band became more popular the crowds increased and eventually they had to find a larger venue at Kimbell's Ballroom in the heart of Southsea. We supported the new venue, but we lads preferred the original atmosphere where bodily contact with the opposite sex was almost unavoidable! The Railway Hotel would later close its doors to the public and stand derelict for many years before being demolished in 2000 to make way for new houses.

On alternate Saturdays during the football season, before going to Fratton Park, a group of us would often take a stroll to Portsmouth city centre and to the Commercial Road area. Here, in the 1960s, on the corner of Arundel Street and Commercial Road, stood the very impressive store of LDB (Landport Drapery Bazaar), now Allders. On the first floor in a large cafeteria area a live rock and roll band would be performing – this was free of charge, but you had to purchase a bottle of Coke, a coffee or maybe a slice of cake to be able to sit down at the tables and listen to the music.

Another free admission in the mid-1960s was to the popular Parade Hotel in Southsea. Here we would dance to the sounds of the Steve Kingsley Disco; this was in a small room at the rear of the pub – it certainly gave us 'bodily contact' with the females, as the area was often very crowded! Steve, like me, was an ardent Pompey fan. We met regularly when the Grosvenor Press Sports and Social Club held their Annual Dinner and Dance. Steve would be our disc jockey in the Gaiety Suite in South Parade Pier, Southsea. I still keep in contact with Steve – his popular disco is still 'on the road' and I should imagine that it must be one of the longest running in Britain.

After leaving the LDB store we would either catch the No. 18 trolleybus to Goldsmith Avenue or more than likely walk the several miles to Fratton Park. If he was not already with us, we would call in at Fernhurst Road to pick up David Copus. We usually found time before the 3 p.m. kick-off to visit a small shop in nearby Winter Road called Tony Collett's Music Shop. Here we were in our element as this establishment was also a model railway shop and at that time David had a thriving 00-gauge layout in a spare bedroom. He would ponder over purchasing one of the latest locomotives or maybe a selection of Tony Collett's own superb card and plastic wagons and vans that he designed himself. While David was in deep contemplation, Eddie and I would be glancing at the latest top ten pop chart and flicking through the latest 45rpm record releases. We were aware that Tony had a passion for railways as he had often mentioned this during previous visits. On one occasion we were taken into his garden at the rear of the shop to discover to our surprise that he had a working 3in-gauge steam locomotive on a length of elevated track. Tony Collett also had a collection of ex-BR steam locomotive name-plates, which we always marvelled at; he kept them discreetly hidden in his shop. It seemed we were always well treated by Tony, probably because he banked at the North End branch of the National Provincial Bank where Eddie worked, and they spoke quite often on the subject of steam railways.

Football took up a considerable part of our leisure time, and other sports tended to fade into the background. In the summer months, however, following the fortunes of Hampshire

County Cricket Club provided not only me but also many of my trainspotting companions with a peaceful and relaxing game played in pleasant surroundings at the Burnaby Road ground in Portsmouth. As it happened, the main railway tracks in and out of Portsmouth Harbour station were situated on an elevated section overlooking the cricket ground. It goes without saying that our cricket score-cards often included a list of steam engine numbers which we would pick out with the aid of binoculars. Saturdays and Sundays were the most exciting as there would inevitably be a 'Hall', 'Grange' or a Mogul heading into the station with an eight- or ten-carriage excursion from the Midlands or West of England.

We did not fanatically support Hampshire CCC – probably only watching two or three matches in Portsmouth during the season, but nevertheless, like the football, we followed their results with interest. I recall the likes of Derek Shackleton, Roy Marshall and the legendary Barry Richards – I saw the last mentioned score a brilliant 206 runs against Notts in 1968. At that date we still combined our railway and cricket interests but sadly steam-hauled trains had finished in Portsmouth by 1967.

We normally visited Hayling Island by train from Fratton via Havant; in the late 1950s this would set you back the sum of 2*s* 10*d*. Occasionally, especially on a hot summer's day, we would choose to use the 'other route'. This entailed taking the small ferry across the mouth of Langstone Harbour from the Eastney district of Portsmouth, and for us adventure-seeking lads it usually proved to be a trip on which we would meet up with girls who were

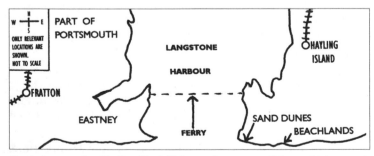

Our 'other route' to Hayling Island. This was via a very small ferry which we took from the Eastney district of Portsmouth.

also looking for some adventure. Hayling Island was renowned for its sandy beaches, and its secluded sand dunes provided us teenagers with some unprecedented romps, and hold some very fond memories. All this combined with a visit to the funfair at Beachlands and the long walk back to the ferry provided us with some gentle relaxation away from the hectic, self-imposed timetables of trainspotting.

I will never forget one particularly scary crossing of Langstone Harbour. My friends and I had become friendly with a buxom girl called Hilary Thomas who resided in Devonshire Square, Southsea, and happened to attend our youth club. Her parents owned a house-boat adjacent to Eastney ferry pontoon and also a small wooden boat, so when she offered her services to ferry us across the harbour to Hayling Island, we naturally accepted. We were about two-thirds of the way across when the boat started to take in water. Being a non-swimmer I became a bit concerned but a bucket and some other objects were quickly put to use and helped to bail us out! Luckily we reached dry land safely. Although trainspotting was our number one hobby, it goes without saying that certain members of our group fancied Hilary, and a visit to her houseboat was always looked forward to in great anticipation!

When visiting Roger Emptage in Exeter Road, Southsea, the sound of a trumpet often echoed from the downstairs front-room, especially during the early evening. This was Roger's father Stanley practising – he played professionally with the Benny Freedman Band. They were a very well-known band, and he played with them from the late 1940s until the mid-1960s. Stanley also gave music lessons from the confines of his house attic, which confused us when visiting since we could hear the trumpet but not see where it was coming from!

As well as attending rock and roll concerts or hearing groups in local clubs and public houses, we used to buy records. In the 1950s we had 78rpm records, but these gave way to 45rpm singles and the 33rpm long-players. We all had our favourite artist or groups, Eddie Rooke's was Buddy Holly and the Crickets, while I took a great interest in American rock and roll singer Ricky Nelson. Whenever he had a new release I would try to buy it from Titmus's Music Shop in Arundel Street or upstairs in the music section of the Co-op Store in Fratton Road. It was not just a passing interest.

Ricky Nelson was my teenage idol and my personal collection of twenty-one singles, twenty-five long-playing and a selection of extended-play records, together with cassettes and videos, proves that point. We bought programmes from concerts that we attended, and in later years they were much sought after by collectors.

The 1960s pop music era was something that we all know about, and for us Portsmouth trainspotters, rock and roll music was never very far away, especially as Eddie Rooke would take his transistor radio with him on many of our trainspotting trips, and naturally tuned in to Radio Luxembourg. Apart from Portsmouth Guildhall, the Savoy Ballroom on Southsea seafront, opposite South Parade Pier, was the 'in place' to see and dance to all the top rock and roll bands, such as the Crickets, The Beatles, The Yardbirds, The Nashville Teens, The Merseybeats, Gerry and the Pacemakers, The Hollies, Nero and the Gladiators and The Kinks, to name but a few. The Liverpool Sound was with us and numerous bands from that city enjoyed their stint at the Savoy. The manager of this popular establishment was a Mr George Turner, whose claim to fame was to have booked The Beatles for a fee of just £50, and to have charged admission of a mere 5s to see them live on stage! Sunday 7 April 1963 is etched in my memory as the day the 'Fab Four' appeared at the Savoy. This was before they became famous and before they had made an impact on the British pop charts. George also had the distinction around that time of booking another up-and-coming band to appear at the Savoy for a fee of just £75 – these were the Rolling Stones. Unfortunately, the Savoy has become a casino today.

In the mid-1960s an exciting new sound known as R&B (rhythm and blues) began spreading rapidly. It certainly converted some of my friends away from the rock music they had grown up with from the mid- and late 1950s. The Birdcage at Eastney was probably the most popular venue for this new sound. A few of the exponents of this type of music who appeared were Georgie Fame and the Blue Flames, Long John Baldry with Julie Driscoll, and Chris Farlowe. Apart from these, American blues artists were regularly performing in Portsmouth at this date and some of those that I saw were John Lee Hooker, Jimmy Reed and Champion Jack Dupree. The last mentioned appeared at the Star Inn, Lake Road in a rather small upstairs room, creating a great atmosphere in his one-off visit from the States. A garage now exists on the former site of the Birdcage.

We also enjoyed folk and skiffle music, as it gave us an opportunity to sit down, relax and appreciate a different kind of easy-listening sound. I probably enjoyed this type of music more than my friends. Eddie was a true rock and roll fan and for him most other types of music were always second-best. Two names spring to mind from the local 1960s folk scene, these being Jon Isherwood and Pat Nelson, with 'Cosham Cowboy' Len Betts getting in on some of the later acts and doubling up as a compère. It was always a pleasure to visit that marvellous building, the King's Theatre in Albert Road, Southsea. During 1960 we saw the 'skiffle king' Lonnie Donegan, supported among others by that popular country duo of Miki and Griff. Trad jazz was another popular sound of the 1960s which I remember many of our youth club female friends being attracted to. Neither Eddie nor I were interested at that time, but that changed for me in the 1970s and 1980s when I frequented jazz clubs with my friend Les Forward. We used to visit the Great Harry at Warsash, the Dolphin Hotel at Botley and two marvellous venues in Portsmouth, the Air Balloon and the India Arms. At the last two I often saw one of my Grosvenor Press workmates, Bob Jenkins, who was an expert on the clarinet, not to mention consuming numerous pints of ale during his band's performance!

There were many pure rock and roll bands, usually three- or four-piece outfits, that played live music on the local circuit in the 1960s and later. Many would begin their gig with an instrumental, a Shadows or a Ventures number, and I expect they were all hoping to hit the big time. Some of the bands I had the pleasure to listen and dance to were the Teenbeats, Johnny Devlin and the Detours, the Rivals, Terry Franks and the Avalons, Mike Anger and the Wild Ones, Chris Ryder and the Southern Sounds, Karl and the Rapiers, the Action and the Vagabonds. I wonder if any of these still perform today, as they must be staring retirement age in the face?

Eddie Rooke, David Copus and I once attempted to record our own songs onto tape. The results were, to say the least, rather crude and our lack of musical knowledge was evident! It was in the early 1960s when I felt an urge to purchase a brand-new acoustic guitar from a shop called Musical Homes in Fratton Road for the sum of £5. I could play piano but that was my only knowledge of music at this time, so this was a new adventure for me. Eddie, influenced by the pop groups of the day, decided that drums would be his forte, but had to make do with his mum's upturned biscuit tin and china tea cups with teaspoons used as drum-sticks. David had the use of a kazoo! To say that any of us ever mastered these 'instruments' would be completely wrong, but it was all great fun putting together recording sessions in Eddie's mum's front-room. She must have wondered what was going on as most of the time was spent in fits of laughter. Obviously none of us took our music seriously!

Tunes were vaguely recognisable but the words were amended to refer to names chosen from the local telephone directory, as mentioned earlier. Many of these tapes have been lost over time, but a few remain to remind us of our futile attempts to record our own songs. It was just another pastime that gave us pleasure when we were not trainspotting.

The Theatre Royal, Portsmouth, a unique Victorian theatre converted from the Landport Hall in 1856. The new theatre was remodelled in 1880 by C.J. Phipps. In 1980 the new Theatre Royal Trustees Ltd purchased the theatre and it is now being restored. (*Drawing by kind permission of the New Theatre Royal*)

There always seemed to be something to amuse us or keep us out of mischief. As previously mentioned, walking was one of these, and it inevitably produced a thirst. We would stop at Southsea coffee bars such as Delmonico's, or the Keyhole in Osborne Road. At Delmonico's coffee lounge there would nearly always be the relaxing background sound of Ray Charles – on LP – as we consumed our drinks. The Keyhole, in contrast, was rather more basic. I would sit at a table with a group of up to six friends for almost an hour, either sipping a cup of coffee or drinking a fizzy drink to the sound of a noisy juke-box belting out all the latest pop numbers. The highlight of our visit would be to insert some coins in the juke-box and listen to the Dave Clark Five singing 'Glad All Over' while we crashed our cups and bottles on the table in unison with the record!

We often visited the cinema in Portsmouth, sometimes twice a week, and it provided us not only with enjoyment but the chance to relax, expecially if we had walked there. In the early 1960s we had twenty-four cinemas to choose from. Sadly, this has declined to four today, brought about by the popularity of television and home videos. Eddie and I had a cinema almost on our doorstep, the Troxy in Fratton Road. The titles of films we saw back in the 1960s are now a bit blurred, but some will always spring to mind – *Robin Hood*, *Conflict of Wings*, and Jerry Lewis in *Rock-a-Bye-Baby*. The Gaumont in Bradford Junction, Southsea, was another of our favourites; like many others it closed and became a bingo hall. There were attempts to re-open it as a concert hall, and American pop group Emile Ford and the Checkmates made an appearance, but it was only a one-off.

Portsmouth theatres included the King's in Albert Road, where I attended many exciting Christmas pantomimes in my earlier years and while still at school was taken with my class by our music teacher to listen to a symphony concert. For the record this was my first and last symphony concert! The Theatre Royal, near the main railway station, was the very first theatre I ever visited, in the company of my parents in the early or mid-1950s. I saw such vintage comedians as Max Miller, 'Cheerful' Charlie Chester, Jimmy Jewell and Ben Warris. Portsmouth citizens should feel proud that these two such architecturally magnificent theatres are still with us today.

21

Strict Parents

My father, George Oliver Harvey, never commented much on my trainspotting adventures, except to say they should not interfere with my work as a compositor at Grosvenor Press. He was always very firm in his actions and I knew where I stood – if I had done wrong I was punished. George was employed for many years as a highly respected and skilled French polisher at Woodhouse's, the large furniture store in Commercial Road, Portsmouth, almost opposite Portsmouth and Southsea station. He could also make by hand furniture such as cabinets and coffee tables, which sported a highly finished surface. He had his own workshop at Woodhouse's and if I was trainspotting at the nearby station I would often visit him and assist whenever I could. Apart from his skill in furniture-making he also travelled on the delivery van with the driver, and if a piece of furniture became damaged in transit he was ready to touch it up with his box of polishes on delivery. I am still the proud owner of a superb glass display cabinet and a bureau that my dad made. All this wonderful skill, yet he was unable to write a letter or even sign his name, such was his upbringing!

Under my Mum's Wing

Whereas the parents of my trainspotting companions took an annual summer holiday to a British seaside resort for a week or two, my mum and dad never indulged in any such luxury. Their summer relaxation and enjoyment consisted of day trips from Portsmouth to such locations as Salisbury market, Brighton or Weymouth on a Royal Blue or Southdown coach. I recall that several weekends a year, during the summer months, I was 'farmed off' to my auntie's house in Eastleigh. It made a welcome change of scenery for me, and as her house was within walking distance of the main Waterloo to Southampton railway line, needless to say, the majority of my weekend was spent trainspotting.

With my mother being totally dedicated to bringing up her son properly, I feel that she over-indulged me in her efforts to ensure that I had everything I needed. She probably tried to love me too much, and consequently when I should have been standing on my own two feet she was always there to help me. It was certainly a shade embarrassing for me whenever any of my railway pals visited my house. This brings me to mention the front-room, a room which they always kept in immaculate condition. It had a brand-new red moquette three-piece suite, lush deep-pile carpet, a highly polished coffee table and expensive curtains. The windows were cleaned religiously every Monday. All this luxury, yet I was never allowed access to it on my own! Eddie Rooke, my closest friend, had the privilege of only one visit to this room, and this was over a period of eight years!

My parents took great pride in their appearance, and of course mine as well. A scruffy head of hair, unpolished shoes or a tie out of place would not be tolerated. I was instructed to visit the hairdresser's every two weeks to ensure that the short back and sides image was maintained. As you know from previous chapters, my hairdresser was a Mr Crockett in St Mary's Road. I needed to be rather discreet in my conversations with him as I and my trainspotting friends sometimes used to telephone him and render a little ditty! Saturday mornings were usually set aside for a 'dome scrape' and the small waiting area was always full to bursting. To help pass the time I would read comics such as the *Dandy*, the *Beano* and, my favourite, the *Eagle*. Background music was provided in the form of *Saturday Club* on the radio, belting out all the latest pop records along with interviews with British and American rock and roll artists, and the host was Brian Matthew. In the summer of 1962, waiting my turn for a short back and sides, I had the sudden inspiration to have my hair extremely closely cropped – I think they called it a 'crew cut'. When I returned home and was confronted by my parents I was given a right telling off for not consulting them first! Within six weeks I had reverted back to my original style. Goodness knows what they would have said if I had opted to have a 'DA' hair style, which was all the rage with the rockers of the 1960s. This style was conspicuous as it resembled the rear of a duck!

It was not until I was nineteen that I had the pleasure of wearing my first suit. Even though I had saved up my pocket money and was capable of choosing a suit myself, my mother insisted that she accompany me to Burton's in Commercial Road, Portsmouth to make sure that I purchased wisely! My new-found image, a blue suit that included a waistcoat, coupled with a white shirt and a plain red tie (true Pompey colours), was aired at the Savoy Ballroom, Southsea on many weekends! The 1960s saw the introduction of winkle-picker shoes, and I fell into the trap of wearing them – something that I regretted in later years. Those pointed-toe shoes left me with distinct discomfort to my feet! Returning to suits, in the 1960s you couldn't purchase a suit 'off the peg', they were all 'made to measure', and the outlets would either be Burton's or John Collier's in Commercial Road. Invariably, the suit included a waistcoat as they were a popular acquisition in those days.

No matter how many trainspotting trips I undertook, and how many days that I was away from home, I was always greeted on my return with a generous helping of mum's home-made goodies. My favourite was her apple pie or baked apple. When I lived in Fifth Street, apples were easily forthcoming as there was a substantial supply from our tree in the garden. Jam and cream sponge cake and fresh fruit salad was another treat, usually reserved for Sunday tea. I spent most Sundays visiting locomotive depots, on the popular Sunday excursion trains that I have already mentioned. If I wasn't trainspotting I would attend Sunday school, and this would be followed by an enormous roast dinner at noon.

Homes in the 1960s were generally heated by a coal fire, and my parents' house was no exception. I have many memories of this helping to dry the washing and keeping the chimney sweep employed, and spending a winter's evening with the moggy curled up on the hearth rug in front of the fire and using mother's extending brass toasting fork to provide hot toast for tea. All this while listening intently to *Down Your Way* on the radio. Oh, so many reminiscences! Although I cannot help but think back to those happy, carefree days devoid of television, videos, computers and mobile phones, when I was a victim of my mother's devotion, I wonder if other parents treated their children with the same love and respect?

22

A Tartan Escapade

The reminiscences in this book primarily portray my own trainspotting adventures (either alone or with my friends), but I feel that I must include a condensed version of an extraordinary nine-day trip to the North-east of England and Scotland which my close friends, David Copus and Frank Allen, undertook in July 1962. Unfortunately, I could not join them as my diary had already been booked. I have concentrated on some of the incidents during this escapade rather than the engine shed visits.

David and Frank used a seven-day 'Freedom of Scotland' ticket costing £6 6s and forty-five locomotive depots were successfully 'bunked', although David did carry his customary wad of 'used' permits just in case they came face-to-face with a difficult shed foreman.

David persuaded his father to fund his ticket and travel costs to and from Newcastle, while Frank worked during part of his school holidays as a waiter in a Southsea guest-house for the sum of £3 10s, plus tips, for an eighty-hour week. Their first thrill was to travel on the 'Queen of Scots' express between Kings Cross and Newcastle, albeit hauled by a 'Deltic' diesel. As a forerunner to their Scottish visits they toured the north-east, taking in on Sunday 22 July seven locomotive depots, at which, surprisingly, they needed to use four official permits.

Accommodation on the first night was in a communal room in a guest-house in the centre of Newcastle, costing them 10s each. They shared the room with some complete strangers who arrived soon after midnight in a state of total inebriation, and proceeded to play cards noisily until dawn. Needless to say, neither David nor Frank got much sleep! It was probably this experience that led them to look for alternative sleeping arrangements courtesy of British Railways for the remainder of their adventure.

To help their aching bodies, they snatched sleep during the day while travelling between stations. To awaken them from this and their overnight waiting-room slumbers and overnight train journeys, David took along a large old-fashioned alarm clock complete with brass bells on top of its face and with powerful gongs. This would make sure that they did not sleep through any scheduled train stops or miss any connections. On many occasions during their escapade, the clock caused great amusement to local passengers, and no doubt many of them viewed the two trainspotters as examples of eccentric Sassenachs!

I have mentioned previously those 'Play Up Pompey' gummed labels that we railway and football supporters distributed, not only at visiting football grounds but also at many locations on the way to football matches, as well as postings during our trainspotting trips. This trip was no exception: those gummed labels found their way to countless locations in Scotland, including the ferries of the Western Isles. One particular road sign at Wick came in for quite some punishment. They also left their mark in the fish and chip shops which were the usual source of David and Frank's main meal of the day; and the final handful was stuck on the tenders of steam locomotives at both Carlisle depots!

With the exception of that sleepless night in Newcastle, one overnight train between Edinburgh and Aberdeen and their return overnight train from Edinburgh to Kings Cross, their nights were generally spent in station waiting-rooms on long, hard wooden seats. They had become masters of the night-time accommodation game, having learned from previous experiences. They knew that if they arrived at stations in large cities like Glasgow or Edinburgh well after midnight, they would be rewarded with a trouble-free sleep, as any drunks or tramps would have already been moved on by local police. David left his mark on many of these seats with the gummed label legend.

On the fourth day of David and Frank's hectic timetable they found for the first time, following their 'bunking' of Fort William depot, that they had some time on their hands. Being in need of a decent meal, they went into a small café and eagerly tucked into an enormous breakfast of sausage, egg, bacon, tomatoes and fried bread washed down with unlimited cups of tea, which cost them the sum of just 1s 10d each. At some point Frank happened to comment that David's feet were starting to smell. David retaliated by removing one of his smelly socks and waving it in front of Frank's face, causing a major upheaval in the crowded café. The proprietor ejected them from his establishment, and they went leaving behind some upturned teacups, saucers and cutlery on the floor, not to mention the remains of the greasy breakfast splattered on David's trousers – something he kept reminding Frank of for the remainder of their adventure! This was just one memorable incident from their nine-day 'Tartan Escapade', but apart from these kinds of antics they would remember those gummed labels, the sleeping rough, the constant dodging of shed foremen, and a rigorous self-imposed schedule, as a result of which they managed to take home to Portsmouth over fifty black and white photographs from their travels.

While in Scotland they saw steam classes ranging from 'Y9' 0–4–0 saddle-tanks to 'A4' Pacifics and it being 1962 they witnessed many dying classes of motive power, soon to be replaced by the diesel and the multiple-unit trains. David told me about the dream that he had where he purchased a 'Y9' class and took it back to Fratton depot to run it on the Hayling Island branch line – well, it was only a dream! Undoubtedly, this class was his favourite tank design on this trip and he was delighted not only to see but also photograph the remaining 'Y9' 0–4–0 saddle-tanks, Nos 68104 and 68117 at Kipps depot (65E), 68095 at St Margarets (Edinburgh) depot (64A) and 68101 at Dunfermline depot (62C).

Not only did they contrive to sleep overnight in waiting-rooms, but also in railway carriages after they had been deposited in the sidings! This was put into practice on their late-night arrival at the terminus station of Kyle of Lochalsh, their ploy being to retreat to separate toilets until the carriages had emptied of passengers and been shunted into the adjacent station sidings. You could say that it was a kind of 'en suite' B&B accommodation, courtesy of British Railways, that proved to be both comfortable and quiet! Just before 4.50 on the next morning, Wednesday 25 July, David's trusty alarm clock came into its own. They hastily ate a packet of crisps washed down with some Tizer. They were planning to catch the 5.10 a.m. MacBrayne ferry from the adjacent Kyle of Lochalsh

Pier to Mallaig. Luckily, the loud gongs on the alarm clock did not arouse the attention of any nearby railwaymen!

David and Frank were very lucky with the weather and had warm pleasant, sunny days, until Saturday 28 July when they woke up (thanks to the alarm clock) in Edinburgh (Princes Street) station waiting-room. They found that inclement weather had arrived with a vengeance − it was absolutely pouring with rain and the dull grey sky suggested it was set in for the day. But a little drop of rain would not blunt their enthusiasm to carry on with their trainspotting visits; after all, they were proud owners of the famous 'Pak-a-mac'. Frank has a particular memory of this day because David's plastic mac had been sabotaged, as they discovered when it was unfolded, by a sticky stale cake that smelt awful! Poor David, with those smelly socks, the remains of a breakfast still evident on his trousers, and now this. He was becoming rather unpleasant to know!

Towards the end of their mammoth trainspotting escapade, they found some brief moments to sit down on a station platform seat and reflect on their visits so far. Their timetable, worked out weeks in advance, had been a plan of great precision, and on the ninth and final day it dawned upon them that they had not encountered any late trains. All their connecting trains were 'on time' and unlike today's railway system in Great Britain they found no cancellations. To cope with some tight schedules they indulged in the luxury of a taxi to convey them to or from the station or depot, giving them extra breathing space instead of having to dash to catch the train.

Having the luxury of a reserved seat was a delight on the homeward-bound overnight train between Edinburgh Waverley and London (Kings Cross), giving them the chance for a long period of much-needed sleep. The seats cost 2s. With the customary Tizer and Smith's crisps to keep them company during the early stages of the journey (having previously visited a fish and chip shop), their thoughts turned to a good night's kip, but not before they totalled up their catch for the nine days − they had noted no fewer than 1,735 British Railways steam locomotives!

It would, no doubt, be utter bliss to arrive back home in Portsmouth the next day and return to normal living hours, normal food, a soak in a Radox bath and a proper bed to sleep in, all after having to confront what must have been two sets of very anxious parents awaiting their safe return. This was truly an extraordinary trainspotting trip that I regret to this day that I was unable to take part in. This trip and many others like it were happy days for these easily pleased teenagers who found that the hobby of trainspotting took in a much wider spectrum of events than they ever envisaged when they first took notebook and pencil to the railway station.

23

Another Camping Fiasco

Following our initial failure to combine a trainspotting trip with camping at Barnstaple in 1961, Eddie and I decided that we would give it another try in early June the following summer, with an adventure taking in Wales and a part of Lancashire. From our previous experience we had learned it would be to our advantage to acquire sleeping-bags and a small paraffin stove, and these were duly purchased. But another important addition, having the tent waterproofed, we totally ignored and as a result we were made to suffer. At this time Eddie was still the proud owner of WTP 977 – a Lambretta L1 150 scooter. Once again I rode pillion, my main job being to give Eddie directions as I was entrusted with the map. We set off from Eddie's house on the Saturday morning in bright sunshine, looking forward to visiting engine sheds along our route. Our first refreshment stop was at that famous location of Stonehenge in Wiltshire, where we took a few photographs. The next locations we passed through were Devizes, Chippenham, Malmesbury, Tetbury and Stroud, before coming to Gloucester, where we took the road to Cardiff, arriving late in the afternoon. As it was the cherry season, we had made a brief stop at Gloucester and bought a couple of pound bags.

The weather was still warm and sunny as we set up our tent. The site was at Porthkerry west of Cardiff; although it was a camping site we only saw two other tents. Nobody approached us for any fees, and we got the impression that the site was now closed. Nevertheless, we pitched our tent and then made our way to nearby Cardiff to buy the inevitable bag of chips, and visited an off-licence where I spoilt myself and bought a quart bottle of the local Brain's brown ale. Later that evening, listening to Radio Luxembourg on Eddie's transistor radio, I had my usual – a packet of crisps, some local ale and, for afters, a Hales apricot fruit pie from my haversack. Then, to finish off, some of those cherries – definitely a night-cap to make me sleep!

The next morning we began our engine shed visits early, but not before washing down a stale cheese sandwich with a few gulps of Brain's. We had planned to work our way through to Oswestry to end our second day, though we did not have a single permit to visit any of the planned depots. Our first 'bunking' was Barry scrapyard where nineteen steam, all Western Region, were noted awaiting their fate. Moving on the short distance to Barry depot (88C) we thought that we had met the foreman, but luckily for us the railwayman turned out to be a most friendly engine driver who gave us details of a 'stored' '5400' class 0–6–0 pannier tank, No. 5416, out of sight at the back of the engine shed. Amid an array of tank locomotives at this depot we noted solitary 'Hall' class 4–6–0 No. 4956 *Plowden Hall*.

Heading eastwards we travelled next into Cardiff to visit Cardiff (Canton) depot (88A); being a Sunday morning the building and yard were full of steam locomotives, and there was no sign of that man! Of the forty-nine 'on shed' there were two withdrawn 'King' class 4–6–0s, Nos 6003 *King George IV* and 6024 *King Edward I*. Following the coast road we came to Newport (Ebbw Junction) depot (86A). Both of us had visited this depot previously and we knew from past experience that if you had no permit you needed to pass the gateman's hut at speed. This we did and looking back over my shoulder I could see a rather irate gateman frantically waving his arms at our illegal entry. Having parked the scooter out of his sight, we successfully 'bunked' the depot, noting seventy-five steam. The same method was used to depart and once again a very annoyed gateman was helpless in stopping us. The same chap was probably on duty when on one of our previous visits a taxi driver was given orders to ignore the gateman and speed towards the depot building!

Hereford depot (86C) went without any hitches and we noted twenty-five steam, including 'County' class 4–6–0 No. 1024 *County of Pembroke*. Our route then took us to Craven Arms depot. This was quite a small four-lane sub-depot of Shrewsbury where four steam were 'on shed', Nos 4617, 42182, 48369 and 48761. Passing through Church Stretton we soon arrived at Shrewsbury depot (89A). Here we witnessed thirty-five steam, which included two 'Hall' class 4–6–0s stored pending further use. Leaving the town, we took the A5 to Oswestry where, on our arrival, we located a small and cosy-looking café near the railway station. Both of us were now in need of a meal and some sleep, but before the latter we had another engine shed visit. Having consumed a very generous mixed grill which included several mugs of tea, all at an inclusive cost of 2s each, we set off feeling quite refreshed to visit Oswestry depot (89D). We were greeted with the sound of two '1400' class 0–4–2 tank engines, Nos 1434 and 1438, letting off steam in the yard. We noted fifteen steam 'on shed'.

It was now very late in the evening and we urgently required a place to pitch our tent. We noted what looked like an ideal piece of grass adjacent to a single-line railway track, not too far from the depot. We quickly set up the tent and looked forward to an uninterrupted night's relaxation. Eddie, having had the responsibility of getting us safely to this location, must have been in dire need of sleep. Despite our tiredness, we still had enough energy to stay awake to listen to Radio Luxembourg for an hour or so.

All went well until 5.30 next morning, when we were awoken by a very loud voice. Peering out of the tent, we saw in the distance a farmer striding towards us, shouting 'Get out of my field'! We had both suffered a similar experience the previous year, so you can imagine we made another extremely quick demolition job of the tent; the sleeping-bags and haversack were gathered up in a bundle under my arms and, quick as a flash, we departed. At this point we noticed that the angry farmer was carrying a shotgun! Having been woken up so early, we continued our journey towards Blackpool, where we hoped our third camping site would bring us some better luck. We repacked all our camping gear once we were at a safe distance from the illegal field.

Taking the road to Wrexham, travelling via Chirk and Ruabon, we paused in a lay-by and ate a breakfast of custard creams and Tizer. Then, as the shops were just opening, a further supply of cherries was added to our haversacks. First engine shed 'bunked' was Croes Newydd depot (89B), noting twenty-three steam including '4300' 2–6–0s Nos 7302, 7313 and 7314, but the most unlikely sighting was Eastern Region 'B1' class 4–6–0 No. 61239 of Gorton (9G). On our journey we passed Bank Hall depot (27A), where several LMS steam were to be seen, but we did not make a visit. Before our visit to Preston depot (24K) we stopped briefly to consume the half-pound

I was pillion passenger and navigator on Eddie Rooke's Lambretta scooter on this 600-mile trainspotting trip of Wales, the Borders and Lancashire. We pitched our tent at three locations, Porthkerry, Oswestry and Blackpool.

bags of cherries bought earlier. We noted that the depot had recently been badly damaged by fire; its charred remains and supports still held the roof intact, although it looked far from safe. We successfully completed our visit without any foreman in sight and for us 'southerners' the joy of seeing eleven 'Patriot' class 4–6–0s at one location was memorable but sad. They were all by this date 'out of use' and destined for scrapping at Derby Works.

On the outskirts of Blackpool we actually set up tent at an official camping site on a farm. There was no way we would have a repeat of the previous night. At the farm we bought some eggs, bacon, sausages and milk for our breakfast the next morning. Having had quite a leisurely day so far, we happily set off to enjoy the bright lights and other attractions of the promenade, which for us included visits to numerous pin-tables in the amusement arcades. It was obvious that at some point during our trip we would deposit some of those 'Play Up Pompey' gummed labels – our target was Blackpool Tower! Having eaten ourselves silly with enormous bags of chips at 1s each, we were looking forward to returning to the farm camping site for what we hoped would be a good night's sleep.

Up to this point the weather had been very kind to us, but all that was to change dramatically. We woke up at 5.30 on Tuesday morning and found the tent had started to leak. We tried to stem the flow with newspapers and plastic bags but the rain increased and our efforts were in vain. We exchanged some choice words about why the tent had not been waterproofed. Similar words had been used before on other camping escapades but the truth was we had ignored them! The heavy rain of a violent thunderstorm had completely drenched us and our sleeping-bags. We must have looked a sorry sight as we sat dejectedly with our plastic macs and check caps shielding us from the weather. But one item of attire stood the test – my brown lace-up Tuf shoes – so at least I had dry feet!

At about 6.15 a.m. we used our small paraffin stove to cook ourselves egg, bacon and sausages – not an easy task in the inclement weather. Afterwards we ate the remainder of our cherries.

We had planned to visit a succession of engine sheds on the return journey to Portsmouth but because of our soaking we decided to make it home as quickly as possible, leaving Blackpool in pouring rain at 8 a.m. with only our crash helmets and plastic macs as protection. We used the M6 motorway, heading south towards Stoke-on-Trent, where we found ourselves a well-patronised transport café. Here we stopped for baked beans on toast and large mugs of tea. When Eddie spotted a pin-table he decided to try his luck, and having invested several shillings, his reward was a free packet of ten cigarettes. As neither of us smoked we contrived to have a spot of fun at the café entrance. Putting all the cigarettes in my mouth, Eddie then lit them up. For those lorry drivers and motorway users visiting the café we must have seemed a bit weird. A photograph of the event was taken and very quickly the cigarettes were deposited in the rubbish bin!

We arrived home in Portsmouth later that day and by now we were feeling quite relieved that, considering the terrible weather conditions that had prevailed for the greater part of the homeward journey, our trip had been safely negotiated. We made one more 'cherry stop' between Northampton and Newbury to satisfy our needs on what had been a most interesting and eventful 600-mile trainspotting trip on the back of a scooter. To relieve the tension in his legs from sitting in one position during the journey between Stoke-on-Trent and Portsmouth, Eddie from time to time would stand up while travelling at speed! To other road users it must have looked very odd, not to mention the fact that if he had lost his balance, the consequences could have been unthinkable.

It was unfortunate that the final day did not end as planned. It left two very weary, rain-soaked trainspotters cursing the British weather. But if we had previously waterproofed the tent, the story would no doubt have had a less damp finale!

24

St James's Park via JAP 591

Our football excursions from Portsmouth were in the main either by rail or coach, but I remember one particular match vividly not only for the match itself but also for the chain of events that led to us travelling by a combination of scooter, car and being towed. Our destination was St James's Park, the home of Newcastle United Football Club. Portsmouth FC had begun the 1962–63 season reasonably well, having gained promotion from the old Division Three as Champions the previous season. About six days before the match, which was on Saturday 25 August, Eddie Rooke and I decided to get in touch with one of our ex-Portsmouth trainspotting pals, Trevor 'Haggis' Robson, who had moved from Chelsea Road, Southsea, to Bath in Somerset because of work commitments. Trevor had relatives living near Newcastle and it was suggested that the three of us could visit them en route to the football match. Trevor lost no time in contacting his relatives and arranged for us to look in briefly.

Eddie and I set out from Sandringham Road, Fratton, on the sunny mid-afternoon of Friday 24 August on his trusty blue Lambretta. I rode pillion, giving him route directions via Winchester to Reading, Berkshire. This was where we had arranged to meet Trevor, as he would be motoring from Bath to Reading. Even though it was not a train trip, I persisted in taking with me my usual items of attire – the plastic mac, cloth cap and of course that well-worn pair of Tuf shoes. In my haversack as well were the Pompey gong and a large supply of 'Play Up Pompey' gummed labels from David Copus, to be displayed at random between Portsmouth and Newcastle!

After meeting Trevor at the entrance of Reading General railway station, Eddie parked the scooter in an adjacent car park and we transferred to Trevor's grey Ford Popular car, JAP 591. We left Reading late on Friday afternoon and eventually joined the A1 heading north towards Yorkshire, our route being via Newark, Doncaster and Wetherby. The conditions were sunny and warm, ideal in fact, and the road seemed anything but busy. All went as planned until Langthorpe, about 10 miles south of Ripon, when JAP 591 started to play up. After several prolonged bouts of spluttering and juddering it eventually came to a standstill. Before it came to a halt, we had been constantly refilling the radiator with water from a container that Trevor kept in the boot. We were on a fairly busy main road so Eddie and I helped to push the sick car into a lay-by, where Trevor telephoned the Automobile Association for assistance. Much to their credit, they arrived on the scene very quickly and then proceeded to tow us via the B6265 road for a distance of almost 10 miles to a garage forecourt in Ripon, but it was too late when we arrived to consult the garage mechanics or any other staff.

Darkness was now upon us and we had no option but to spend the night in the relative comfort of the Ford Popular. Once we had been towed into the garage and the AA had informed their mechanic, our first objective was to revitalise ourselves with food and drink. We had only stopped briefly for some liquid refreshments on our journey between Reading and Ripon and we were now feeling rather peckish to say the least. My haversack produced one of my favourite fruit pies and some orange squash. My two companions also tucked into their supply of food and drink. Having refreshed ourselves sufficiently, we decided on a walk to stretch our aching legs. We must have been craving more to eat because when we spotted a fish and chip shop we all bought portions of chips and pea fritters. Our tasty treat was taken back to the car and eagerly devoured! To round off this varied and eventful day, we listened to a session of pop music (Radio Luxembourg) on Trevor's portable Bush radio. With the midnight hour fast approaching and both Eddie and Trevor snoring their heads off, I deemed it safe to remove my Tuf shoes and settle down for a good night's kip.

It was 6.30 on Saturday morning when we stirred. Flecks of bright sunlight woke us up and looking out of the car we were greeted with a clear blue sky and the promise of another warm and sunny day. Trevor's first priority was to contact the garage mechanic to diagnose what was wrong with the car. Quite early in the morning we found

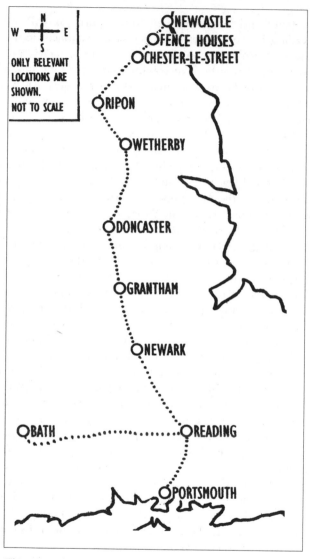

This was our route from Portsmouth to Newcastle, much of which followed the A1. Trevor Robson started off from Bath, and met up with us at Reading. We travelled over 600 miles by scooter and car to watch a football match and do some trainspotting. The lengths that we went to to support our football team 'Pompey' defied belief!

out that a gasket had blown; the repair went ahead and within two hours we were once again back on the road. At Ripon Trevor stayed with the car while Eddie and I took a brisk walk around the town. We refreshed ourselves at a small café with tea and toast, and on our way back to the garage discreetly deposited some of our gummed labels.

JAP 591 was now behaving itself, and just after 11 a.m. we arrived safely at Trevor's Uncle Bob's house in Blind Lane, Chester-le-Street, west of Houghton-le-Spring, County Durham. On our arrival our need for food was satisfied with a 'fry-up' followed by endless sandwiches and hot cups of tea. We were treated like a part of their family, for which we were most grateful. At this point we were roughly ten miles from Newcastle, and we continued in the Ford Popular to Pinewood Street, Fence Houses, where we visited Trevor's family friends, the Hutchinsons. When we showed them the Pompey gong they were amazed and thought it a novel method of making ourselves heard at a football match. Our incessant bashing of the gong soon aroused the neighbours and people stared out of their back windows to find out the cause of the commotion! Before we left we watched television and noted with interest the pre-match details of the Newcastle United v Portsmouth match. We were a little surprised to learn that a group of Pompey supporters had gained entry to St James's Park overnight and had painted the goal posts blue – Pompey's colours!

David Copus and some of his pals were also planning to attend this football match, but their itinerary was by rail from Portsmouth via London (Kings Cross). David had also made some sketchy plans to 'bunk' several engine sheds in that area before the match. Only two weeks previously he and Frank Allen had visited this area, with real permits; needless to say the dates were suitably amended to 25 August 1962 and added to his usual pocketful of used permits! Unfortunately, we did not meet up with David or any of his friends on this trip, but he did in fact 'bunk' Sunderland depot (52G), where he witnessed thirty-four steam locomotives, which included 'Q6' class 0–8–0s Nos 63342, 63345, 63418 and 63456. Also illegally and successfully completed was Consett depot (52K) where a mere twelve steam were 'on shed', including five 'K1' class 2–6–0s introduced as late as 1949, Nos 62002, 62023, 62027, 62050 and 62060.

We found time before the match to visit Newcastle Central railway station, where we marvelled at its magnificent arched roof and its busy platforms. One green-liveried tank engine stood out proudly, the 'station pilot', 'J72' class 0–6–0 No. 68723. We were there only briefly but noted many movements of steam locomotives, including 'A3' class 4–6–2s Nos 60072 *St Gatien* and 60088 *Book Law*, 'V2' class 2–6–2 No. 60913, and named 'B1' class 4–6–0 No. 61019 *Nilghai*, which its shed-plate showed was allocated to Blaydon depot (52C). We also noted several more 'J72' class 0–6–0 tanks including Nos 68736 and 69025. We also had time enough to jot down some diesel locomotives, these being Nos D274, D277, D2045, D2322, D3321, D5099, D5102 and D9008. Oddly enough, we never had any plans to visit any engine sheds in the area.

Even though it was early in the season, the vocal support that Portsmouth FC received was really tremendous; the Portsmouth mascot in his sailor's uniform paraded around the ground before the kick-off, and the Pompey fans in high spirits. Those gummed labels left their mark most cheekily of all, carefully stuck on the back of one unsuspecting home supporter! Countless coaches and many private cars made the long journey north, helping to swell the attendance to just over 35,000. Unfortunately British Railways deemed it unprofitable to run a special train from Portsmouth. The game, however, failed to meet our expectations and the final score was 1–1, Portsmouth's scorer being Tony Barton. The Pompey gong was given an extended airing at this match, causing many comments from the home supporters, made in loud, boisterous voices of which we could only pick up snatches. Their remarks both complimentary and otherwise were taken in good humour.

Motoring south from Newcastle, we soon returned to Trevor's friends' house at Fence Houses, where again we were made most welcome with generous helpings of meat sandwiches, fruit cake and tea. That evening was spent in the house, and for once we were in a relaxed mood. We watched television and this included the sports channel where we saw snatches of the match.

As far as I can recall, Trevor slept in a spare bedroom while Eddie and I used the dining-room floor. After a substantial fried breakfast early the next morning, we thanked Trevor's friends for their hospitality, and set off on the long journey home. But before our departure, the early morning silence of those humble terraced houses in Pinewood Street was rudely broken with four or five hearty bashes on the Pompey gong – signalling our farewell!

JAP 591 behaved impeccably, and the homeward journey via the A1 was uneventful, except for when we stopped off at a café near Stamford, where the remaining gummed labels were discreetly plastered on the tables, chairs and a telephone kiosk! Trevor eventually dropped us off at Reading General railway station entrance and we thanked him for all his efforts and time in transporting us safely. He still had a considerable journey home to Bath. Eddie and I were now reunited with the Lambretta scooter which would take us on the final stage of our 600-mile journey, via Farnham, Liss and Petersfield on almost deserted roads. With the gong safely tucked under my arm and an empty haversack on my back, we made our leisurely way home in bright sunshine. The weather had been kind to us throughout and we had not needed macs and caps. It certainly had been a very memorable three days, a football excursion with a difference, in which JAP 591 had played a large part.

25

A Very Shrewd Transaction

It was probably the increase in railway fares that prompted Eddie Rooke to find alternative modes of transport to enable us to continue our locomotive depot visits, both locally and further afield.

One car I shall never forget was bought by Eddie in the spring of 1963. It was not used on many long-distance trainspotting runs, but it was used extensively as a local runabout car, visiting railway locations such as Eastleigh and Southampton and our local branch line from Havant to Hayling Island. The car in question was a 1937 Austin Seven, registration BDP 922, for which Eddie paid the grand sum of £5 cash to a milkman employed at Walker's Dairy in Guildford Road, Fratton, just fifty yards from my home. It was in a very sorry state when purchased, but the dairy worker assured Eddie that the car was completely functional and roadworthy, and only needed a paint job. Within a few days Eddie and I set about sprucing it up. The original paintwork was mostly blue, but between us we transformed it with an application of bright blue, yellow and black gloss paint, doing the whole job outside Eddie's house in Sandringham Road, Fratton.

For almost a year the Austin Seven was a perfect runner but during a fast run to Petersfield with David Copus, when we achieved a record speed of 92 mph on a downhill stretch of road near Horndean, just north of Portsmouth, the car began to shudder. Looking towards the floor we could see the road beneath us! More holes appeared but despite this Eddie continued to use the car locally for a further four or five months before it completely broke down. He then made a very shrewd transaction. He managed somehow to sell the clapped-out car to a sailor based at Portsmouth Royal Naval Dockyard for the grand sum of £17 cash. Rubber mats were placed over the offending holes and Eddie, being employed at National Provincial Bank, used all his expertise to make a handsome profit of £12!

In the early and mid-1960s only Eddie and Trevor Robson owned cars. David Copus eventually moved up to four wheels when he had the opportunity to buy a small van cheaply from his employers, Portsmouth Water Company at Bedhampton. Its paintwork was a ghastly faded brown, and the PWC inscription on the sides had been partially obliterated by some amateur paintwork. The van had no side or rear windows, and if David transported more than two people, they had to enter through the rear doors. However, David found it very useful for transporting team-mates of Ferndale FC to matches on a Sunday.

26

An Axe Falls and a Tent Rises

As the mid-1960s arrived, a certain Dr Beeching began to wield his axe on our beloved railway system. There were widespread closures of many unprofitable branch lines but, more importantly, secondary rail routes were also biting the dust. My local Hayling Island line was unfortunately one of Dr Beeching's casualties. It seems that Dr Beeching appeared on the scene to sacrifice the romance and glamour of steam-hauled trains to what he envisaged would be an altogether more efficient diesel and electric service.

It was the destruction of our railway that led Eddie Rooke and me to take a last look at as many as possible of those engine sheds threatened with closure and eventual demolition. In some instances it was already too late. We also planned to take a look at some of the Great Western Railway sub-depots and stations in Wales which were under threat of closure, and a selection of larger locomotive depots. As I have already written, the combination of camping and trainspotting always provided some amusing or near-disastrous stories, and this continued well into the 1960s, when we went particularly to Wales and the north-west of England. For us dedicated trainspotters from the south coast, these areas were visited not only for their railways but for some quite stunning scenery.

Deep in the summer of 1965 we set out with the tent, sleeping bags, a small paraffin stove and an extremely well-filled haversack together with my dad's Brownie box camera, on a five-day railway and camping adventure. We saw this as a 'Farewell to standard gauge steam in Wales', although, as you will see, our travels took us much further afield. By now Eddie had already owned a fawn Ford Popular. After our trip to Newcastle in Trevor 'Haggis' Robson's Ford Popular, Eddie had always dreamed of owning his own, and this came true with the purchase of VUU 527 soon after. But this was quickly followed by a blue Ford Anglia (SOE 99). Although these cars were used on some of our trainspotting trips, we still patronised British Rail, as it became known in 1965, still starting many trips from our local station of Fratton.

This trip, however, was in Eddie's Ford Anglia. We set off on Saturday 24 July, hoping not to repeat our previous camping experiences. But we still had failed to waterproof the tent! Did we really think we could travel for five whole days without a decent shower of rain? Nevertheless, we headed to a camp-site near Barry Island, South Wales. It was handy for 'bunking' the nearby Dai Woodham's scrapyard, where we noted 105 redundant BR steam, of which No. 31638 was instantly recognisable, being an ex-Fratton-allocated 'U' class 2–6–0. We were seeing mostly Western Region classes, but a welcome change was to note that two LMS 'Jubilee' 4–6–0s were also present, Nos 45690 *Leander* and 45699 *Galatea*.

Having pitched our tent in a rather deserted camp-site, we motored off to Cardiff to 'bunk' Canton depot, but realising on entry that it had been dieselised, we decided against a visit. Our visit to the gigantic funfair at Barry Island saw us indulge in the pinball tables. Soon after leaving this noisy area we made our usual visit to buy bags of chips, which we ate in the car. On our return to the camp-site there was a change in the weather. There was a heavy thunderstorm with hailstones; on entering the camp-site we saw our tent marooned in a pool of water! There was no alternative but to spend the night in the comfort of the Ford Anglia with packets of crisps for our supper and the usual radio for company. Considering the awful conditions outside, we both enjoyed a reasonable period of sleep. Waking up at 5.50 we saw that the conditions had eased considerably, and after packing the damp tent on the roof-rack of the car we grabbed some food and drink and set off on our travels.

Radyr depot, a former sub-depot of Cardiff (Cathays), was first to be 'bunked'; just a dozen steam were noted, eight of which were 0–6–0 pannier tanks. Moving on through central towards west Wales we were looking for some of those remote former locomotive sheds that we had visited during our 1961 Western Region Rail Rover. Some were under threat of closure but many of the sheds we visited had already bitten the dust. Our scenic route took us to Abercynon, then via the A4054 to Merthyr. We traversed the road across the

Black Mountains to Brecon and then began the long journey westward via Llandovery and Lampeter to the coastal town of Aberayron, eventually reaching Aberystwyth. Here we paused at a small café for fried egg and chips and tea. While at Aberystwyth we 'bunked' the Vale of Rheidol engine shed where we saw two 2–6–2 tank engines. We were glad that we purchased return tickets to Devil's Bridge, a journey of some twelve miles, on the Vale of Rheidol narrow gauge steam railway, as the view from the train was stunning. At one point we were 680ft above sea level. Our return tickets cost us 6s. In later years the small Vale of Rheidol engine shed was demolished, and the three steam locomotives, Nos 7, 8 and 9, were transferred to the main Aberystwyth engine shed, where they still are today.

Next visited was Machynlleth depot, where we saw two 'Manor' class 4–6–0s, Nos 7812 *Erlestoke Manor* and 7819 *Hinton Manor* (both fortuitously now preserved). Our route then took us via the A493 to Towyn, following the peaceful shores of the wide tidal River Dovey against a marvellous backdrop of hills and mountains. It was the time of the day to think about a camping site. Luckily, we spotted one in Towyn and for once everything went as planned. We cooked a reasonable meal on our small stove, drank some orange squash, I removed my smelly Tuf shoes, and we settled down to listen to the radio.

We awoke to a rain-free morning, and after a small cooked breakfast my aim was to purchase a return ticket to Abergynolwyn via Dolgoch Falls, travelling on the Talyllyn Railway, this being one of the many narrow-gauge railways that could be found in Wales. The next stage of our journey was along the A493 coast road via Llwyngwril, then to Penmaenpool, where we learned that the former engine shed had been demolished. We motored through Merioneth amid some beautiful scenery via Trawsfyndd Lake, where we were most surprised to note a double-decker bus stored in a private yard. On close inspection we defined the word 'Southdown'; as this was one of our local green-liveried buses we wondered if the owner had connections with the Portsmouth or West Sussex areas. The former site of Trawsfyndd engine shed was visited, as well as Portmadoc, a former sub-depot of Machynlleth. Using the A497 road via Criccieth, we had a great view of the impressive castle, then continued along the Lleyn Peninsula to

Pwllheli, where we 'bunked' the engine shed, noting only three locomotives, one 'Manor' and two Standards.

It was then along the A499 road to Caernarvon, where we happened to note several steam as we paused at Bangor station, LMS class 5 4–6–0 No. 45184 and Standard class 4 4–6–0 No. 75009. We found out that the depot had closed down earlier that year. While in Bangor we stopped and asked a pretty young lady for directions to the nearest doughnut shop. She was amused by our request and asked us if we were touring, to which we replied 'Yes'. Our offer to take her photograph wearing my trainspotter's cloth cap was eagerly accepted and she gave us our directions. At the shop we stocked up with bags of hot doughnuts to eat later on in our travels.

Having moved on to Llandudno, we 'bunked' the four-lane Llandudno Junction depot where we saw thirty-one steam, including 'Britannia' class 4–6–2 No. 70046. On the turntable was a WD class 2–8–0 No. 90329; also of note were ten LMS class 2 2–6–2 tanks. Leaving Llandudno, we made the pleasant journey along the north Wales coast road to Pensarn via Colwyn Bay. Our camping site was adjacent to the main road, near the town of Abergele, and was easy to find.

Once again it was the usual ritual of setting up the tent, and visiting the wash and brush-up for a welcome soak in soap and water. By this stage of our travels, it was time to wash our smelly socks. Hopefully they would dry overnight; if not we would begin the next day barefoot. I had added the luxury of a piece of cod and some pickled onions to our usual supper, and had some jam doughnuts to follow up with, and of course the usual bottle of fizzy drink. The sounds of Radio Luxembourg saw us both disappear into the land of nod.

We were hoping that the fine weather would once again smile on us. Would we be lucky and avoid a night-time downpour? We were safe, as the next morning we awoke, after an uninterrupted sleep, to bright sunshine and clear blue skies with the promise of another warm, sunny day ahead. Departure from the camp-site was at 7.30 a.m. on Tuesday 27 July. Feeling refreshed after our decent sleep and with clean socks, we happily plodded along to Mold Junction depot (6B) via Rhyl and Prestatyn. There were only ten steam 'on shed', which included two 'Jinty' tanks. As in the majority of the depots visited, these locomotives, being in the twilight of steam, were dirty and grimy, giving a photographer little scope for a decent sharp picture.

Leaving Mold Junction we motored to Birkenhead depot (8H) which we successfully 'bunked', but not without a bit of a fright. There were thirty-seven locomotives noted, of which twenty were '9F' class 2–10–0s. We were a little wary not only of meeting the shed foreman but also because of a large, clearly worded sign at the depot entrance that read 'Guard dogs patrol this area'. We were a bit 'on edge' because of this sign and half expected an angry Alsatian to leap out from behind a '9F' and take a bite out of our legs. Bearing in mind that our visit took place at dusk, we probably, through anxiety, did not see all of the locomotives. On leaving the depot we felt relieved to have come through unscathed and left our mark on the sign with a selection of 'Play Up Pompey' gummed labels!

We repeated the route from a previous scooter trip and travelled via the Mersey Tunnel to Liverpool and then to Blackpool. As young men we were lured by the promenade and famous tower and the endless amusement arcades; and of course there was the attraction of the young women whom Eddie and I were hoping to meet. But we soon forgot about this when what we had been dreading happened: Blackpool welcomed us with an enormous downpour, and it looked set to continue.

Undaunted by the rain, we cheerfully set up our tent at the farm camp-site about 5 miles out of Blackpool that we had used three years before. I reminded Eddie how we had both woken early back then and found ourselves soaking wet in an unwaterproofed tent! 'I didn't think it would happen again,' I said, but Eddie shook his head and refused to answer! Trying to pretend that we would escape a drenching, we bought eggs and sausages from the farm shop and with our small stove cooked a somewhat tasty meal, finished off with the remaining doughnuts. Radio Luxembourg was switched on and despite the damp conditions outside we snuggled up in our sleeping-bags, put on our macs and cloth caps and settled down for what we hoped would be a reasonable night's sleep.

The next morning, Wednesday 28 July, we woke just before 6.45 to find the inevitable – the tent was flooded, including our sleeping-bags. We were cold and damp and feeling rather dejected that the same location had greeted us with a drenching on both visits, we became rather anti-Blackpool. But, as I pointed out to Eddie, 'If only we had waterproofed the tent.' We exchanged a few words but the fact remained that we had not done what we should have done – a bit like 'bunking' an engine shed on two different visits and being nabbed by the foreman both times! Dejected or not, at least this time we had the luxury of the Ford Anglia to deposit the wet tent and sleeping gear into and the joy of having kept our travelling clothes dry overnight in the car. Breakfast was what still remained in our haversacks from the beginning of the trip five days earlier, so that damp morning we enjoyed between us a large tin of apricots in syrup, together with a whole packet of custard cream biscuits. It was lucky that we remembered to bring a tin-opener.

As we sat in the car pondering what to do next, we could see that most of the camp-site was under water and we decided to make a fairly quick journey home. Departing at exactly 8 a.m., we travelled via the M6 motorway, then via Coventry and Northampton, where we made a welcome stop at a transport café for baked beans on toast and tea, taking bars of chocolate away with us to eat on our journey south.

Before departure from the café, a fair number of those infamous gummed labels were discreetly deposited not only on the chairs and tables but also on the menu boards. The legend of our beloved Portsmouth Football Club had once again left its mark! Over the years, thousands of these labels were deposited at random all over England, Scotland and Wales and we must have been cursed by the people that had the job of removing them.

Our route bypassed London, then we joined the A3 road to Portsmouth and arrived home safely without making any further stops. I thanked Eddie and paid him my share of the petrol money. We both agreed on one thing – we would *never* again go camping at Blackpool!

27

The Change-Over

By the end of 1966 we trainspotters saw our beloved steam locomotives fast disappearing from the Portsmouth area. This was the transitional period or change-over when steam and diesel power could be noted working together, more often than not paired together because of a steam or diesel failure while working a passenger train. Southern Region steam at this date would usually be a Standard 4–6–0 or 2–6–0 or a Bulleid Pacific, no doubt leaking steam from all angles because of its run-down state. We dedicated spotters who were still around grasped the opportunity to photograph both species side by side in the depots, stations and yards.

At that time we could not have imagined that many trainspotters, with their cameras, tape recorders and notebooks and their instinctive passion for 'living' steam, would provide in years to come visual evidence of their exploits to audiences young and old all over Britain in the form of illustrated slide shows and photographic displays, accompanied by their accounts not only of the change-over period but also of much earlier years.

The introduction of diesel and electric locomotives and diesel and electric units, and the mass scrappings of steam, severely depressed the majority of us local trainspotters. I, like numerous others, regretted in later years that we did not capture the change-over period on camera as much as we should have done. We thought that steam would survive into the 1970s at least but we were wrong. BR steam locomotives, such as the '9F' class 2–10–0s, with less than ten years' active service, found themselves being sent to the breakers' yards. Not only were steam locomotives disappearing, but also there were numerous closures of branch lines, with the rapid demise of stations, engine sheds, goods sheds, signal-boxes and the lifting of track. In today's world the humble spotter from the 1960s returns to a previous hunting ground to find that it is now a Tesco, or part of a motorway, a housing estate or a car park.

When the winter of 1966 came upon us, many of the close companions who had accompanied me all over the country on trainspotting adventures quietly slipped away from the local railway scene. Some of them moved away from my group of friends since their social activities such as football, cinema and live music were now with non-railway friends. Unknown to me and my close friends, however, some 'breakaway' friends had taken up employment on British Rail, and others had ventured all over the BR system using 'All-line Rail Rovers', photographing the remains of a once-great railway system. Some even travelled overseas in pursuit of steam. These close friendships which we had known had not gone forever, apparently.

My many friends and I have sentimental memories of those final visits to engine sheds where the change-over provided us with a mixture of ancient and modern traction. Even though we knew working BR steam would no longer be part of our lives, it was still an exciting period and a chance for us to obtain steam/diesel scenes on camera. We never tired of 'bunking' depots, because they all had their own individuality. Unfortunately, apart from today's preserved railways, these experiences will never be repeated again. My close friend Doug Willis recently summed it all up.

'The change-over'. Steam assistance was often called upon in the mid-1960s when new diesels 'failed' owing to teething problems. But more often than not the steam locomotive would itself be run-down and leaking steam from all angles, as in this sketch. Some very interesting combinations were to be observed.

Do you remember us visiting Old Oak Common depot in 1960 to find it crammed tight with nearly 120 steam locomotives? The joy and thrill of such a visit was that we would always cop different engines each time we made a visit – perhaps one from North Wales or Cornwall or the West Midlands. They would all be 'on shed' mingling with the local side and pannier tanks and this was the *real fascination* of trainspotting in those days, compared to a visit to one of today's preserved lines, where people inevitably know prior to their visit which locomotives will be seen.

How true!

28

The Sun Sets on the Southern

By summer 1967 only two areas of Britain, the north-west and part of the Southern Region, still had standard gauge steam locomotives working on scheduled timetabled services. I and my friends and other trainspotters who had met over the years on Fratton station footbridge thought it was now time to bring the curtain down on the local railway scene. I decided in early July to witness some of the final Southern Region steam workings by purchasing a local seven-day Runabout Ticket and visit Basingstoke, Winchester, Southampton, Salisbury and Bournemouth, among other locations, to tape-record and photograph this dying species. I had the use of a friend's camera for this but unfortunately never really mastered it. Nevertheless, I did obtain some photographs.

Probably the highlights were the journeys behind steam locomotives destined for withdrawal later on that week. I found it very sad to know that the once famous class of Bulleid Pacifics was to be retired to some scrapyard in South Wales, and this was my final chance to savour the thrill of being steam-hauled on the Southern Region. The runs behind Battle of Britain class No. 34060 *25 Squadron* between Winchester City and Eastleigh, West Country class No. 34004 *Yeovil* on the 7.40 p.m. Bournemouth Central to Waterloo as far as Southampton Central, and the 6.40 p.m. Salisbury to Waterloo as far as Basingstoke hauled by Standard class 4 4–6–0 No. 75074 will always be remembered. My visits to stations were interspersed with 'bunkings' of Eastleigh, Basingstoke, Bournemouth and Salisbury engine sheds, and as my week unfolded I witnessed numerous filthy looking, run-down steam locomotives leaking steam from every conceivable joint owing to their lack of essential repairs. It was indeed a sorry sight.

When Standard class 5 4–6–0 No. 73029 departed from Bournemouth Central station on Saturday 8 July with one of the last steam-hauled passenger trains to London (Waterloo), it had the words 'THE CUNARDER' chalked on its smoke-box door, together with the chalked plea 'DON'T LET ME DIE'. Later that evening I had a foretaste of future motive power when I was diesel-hauled to Eastleigh by '42' class ('Warship') No. D801 *Vanguard*. British Rail ran two 'Farewell to Steam' specials on Sunday 2 July from Waterloo to Bournemouth, both being hauled by 'Merchant Navy' 4–6–2s. This was prior to the third-rail electrification being switched on to accommodate electric-unit trains.

My return to Portsmouth on Sunday 9 July was a very sad day in the diary of a local trainspotter: the final steam train would be departing from Fratton goods yard, the mid-morning 'Empty Carriage Stock' bound for Clapham Junction hauled by class 5 4–6–0 No. 73029 in green livery. Local railway workers at Fratton depot had adorned the complete smoke-box door with 'FAREWELL TO STEAM' and 'PLAY UP POMPEY' chalked in large capital letters. The engine steamed out of the goods yard and under Milton Lane footbridge, constantly blowing its whistle. This procedure, I learned later, was common practice when a driver or fireman was working his very last turn, and the non-stop whistle-blowing would continue until the train had reached its destination!

But there was one final surprise, as later that afternoon Fratton depot was host to a most unusual type of 0–6–0 tank locomotive, probably the first and last time that a 'USA' class had visited Fratton. No. 30072 was the engine; it had finished its duties as shed pilot at Guildford depot and was the final steam to leave there, but on its way to Salisbury via Havant and Eastleigh its small tanks needed replenishing and its coal bunker topping up – which necessitated it visiting Fratton en route. Not only was No. 30072 the final steam engine to leave Guildford but also Fratton. As a final twist to the story this 'USA' tank, after languishing in Salisbury depot yard for several months, was saved from the cutter's torch and purchased by a preservation society. Today we can see it on the Keighley and Worth Valley Railway in Yorkshire.

Several months after the final timetabled steam train ran on the Southern Region, I visited Salisbury depot. At this date it had been recoded from 72B to 70E, and here I saw sixty ex-BR steam locomotives, either waiting to be towed to scrapyards or (on a more pleasant note) awaiting purchase by various preservation societies. The depot, having officially closed on 8 July 1967, was inundated with an influx of locomotives, and as a result the depot staff were reinstated for an additional three months to allow them to prepare the redundant steam locomotives for their final journey to the South Wales scrapyards.

The majority of the 'USA' 0–6–0 tanks were in their working lives allocated both to Southampton Docks depot (71I) and Eastleigh depot (71A). Now many of them were to be found at Salisbury awaiting their fate. Many of the classes at Salisbury displayed 'RESERVED' notices, being sought after by a selection of preservation societies from all over Britain; but for many it was too late. By the end of September they had all gone and consequently low-loaders had to visit the South Wales scrapyards to tow them away by road. The rest is history.

29

A Trainspotter's Farewell

The year was 1968, the date was Friday 19 April. This was the day I set out on my final trainspotting trip. It was a three-day adventure undertaken knowing that Manchester and Carnforth would provide me with glimpses of some of the last working standard gauge steam locomotives on BR. The final steam-hauled BR passenger train would take place on 11 August, but I took the opportunity to visit the last stronghold of British steam, Lancashire, four months before then. The scene that confronted me can only be described as grim and very sad. Of course, I realised even then that numerous preservation societies were coming into being all over Great Britain. Over a period of years they gratefully purchased many of the steam locomotives that had been pushed aside. These societies, groups and individuals would lovingly restore many of these ex-BR iron horses and preserve them in working order for posterity. Some would even be returned to main-line passenger working, this being organised by their respective owners.

I had spotted an advert in one of the monthly railway magazines advertising a three-day rail and coach tour, '2 D 8', organised by the Thames Valley Rail Enthusiasts Association, to take place between 19 and 21 April at an all-in cost of £6 8s, starting from London. Details regarding train times were posted to me in advance and I travelled alone on the Friday evening, departing from Portsmouth and Southsea station at 10.50 p.m.

Although I had on a number of occasions ventured forth on my own to visit engine sheds and stations, travelling solo this time felt different in that it was tinged with an air of sadness that in four months time steam would be extinct from everyday duties on the BR system. I was not alone on the train to Waterloo, as three other local enthusiasts were also participating in the same tour of Manchester. I did not recognise them as 'regulars' from my Fratton station footbridge days, but they obviously knew me and we consequently conversed about the forthcoming tour.

Even though it was my final major trainspotting trip before the demise of steam, I had to drum up the enthusiasm to go through the well-worn rituals of preparing my cloth haversack for the three days ahead. I packed it tight with sufficient goodies and drink, the customary plastic mac, cloth cap and, most importantly, my recently purchased Kodak Coloursnap camera. The last mentioned proved to be a most valuable acquisition as at the end of the tour I had proudly taken seventy-six colour slides.

My three companions and I met up with the remainder of the group of eighteen at the entrance to Platform 12 at Euston station, including the organiser, a Mr A. Shepperd of Ventnor in the Isle of Wight. The overnight train journey to Manchester (Piccadilly) proved uneventful: our group located our reserved seats and my first thoughts were to satisfy my needs of food and drink, which consisted of crisps and a welcome swig of Tizer.

At first light on Saturday morning we found ourselves at Stockport, where I opened the carriage door window to marvel at the truly impressive nineteenth-century railway viaduct which we were about to cross – I had previously delved into its history and found that it contained twenty-seven arches and was reputed to have been built with eleven million bricks! It was near Stockport that we caught our first glimpse of what would be commonplace at the locations we were to visit later that day two '8F' class 2–8–0s in really filthy condition with their numbers just about discernible in charge of freight trains Nos 48170 and 48465.

We arrived at Manchester (Piccadilly) station at the unearthly hour of 4.10 a.m. We were told by our organiser to remain on the train for two hours at its arrival platform and to join the coach, Holt's of Manchester, at the station approach just before 6.30. This was ideal as it afforded us some time to relax before embarking on a mammoth thirteen-hour coach tour of nine locomotive depots which obviously would involve walking a considerable number of miles. I had come prepared, as I wore my Tuf shoes, which after thirteen years of continuous wear had never let me down. In fact they had not even needed their soles replacing, such was their tough leather. Breakfast was taken at a leisurely pace while sitting in the comfort and warmth of the train and this was where my smelly boiled-egg sandwiches caught the attention of my companions. My favourite Hale's fruit pie was soon demolished and then several gulps of Tizer. This kind of menu had been my hallmark over the years as a 'trainspotter's breakfast' and my final trip was to be no different. The coach departed on time and as I recall the group of mainly teenagers was, considering the sadness of the occasion and the earliness of the day, a very happy and friendly bunch.

The first of the nine depots visited was Patricroft (9H), where we noted twenty-seven very grimy steam and a solitary 0–6–0 diesel shunter. Second was Heaton Mersey (9F), where twenty-three out of the thirty steam 'on shed' were '8F' class 2–8–0s. The third visit was to Stockport (Edgeley) (9B). Here we noted just nine 'Black Five' 4–6–0s and three '8F' class 2–8–0s; looking rather out of place amid the work-stained steam was main-line diesel No. D202. Newton Heath (9D) was the fourth visit, where we witnessed the usual classes, including no fewer than twenty 'Black Five' 4–6–0s and 'Britannia' 4–6–2 No. 70023 *Venus* – by this date its name-plates had probably been removed. We did not attempt to visit the substantial diesel depot. The fifth visit was to Bolton (9K), about 10 miles away; the coach driver knew exactly where all our depots were located. We found out that he had taken numerous other groups of railway enthusiasts to these depots and obviously knew the route very well. Twenty-two steam were noted, of which half were Stanier-designed '8Fs'. Out of character , however, was '8F' No. 48773, standing in the yard in immaculate condition waiting to haul a 'special'. This engine had recently returned after service in the Middle East, and had visited Eastleigh Works for an overhaul. It is still with us today in preservation. The sixth depot was Rose Grove (10F), where we saw twenty-nine steam 'on shed', including Standard class 4 4–6–0, Nos 75032 and 75048. In this depot yard we witnessed the remains of locomotives that had been cut up for scrap, class 5 4–6–0 No. 44848 and '8F' 2–8–0 No. 48544 probably being next for the torch. We then went to the Preston area of Lostock Hall (10D), travelling via Blackburn, some 18 miles. The number of steam 'on shed' totalled thirty-two, but about half of these were dumped in sidings waiting to be towed away for disposal. Some of these were class 4 2–6–0s Nos 43006, 43008, 43019, 43027, 43033 and 43106. For the first time on this day we noted two '9F' class 2–10–0s, both in working order Nos 92054 and 92069. From Lostock Hall we travelled via the M6 to our eighth depot at Carnforth (10A). At this depot we noted thirty-five steam of 'Black Five' and '8F' designs, but included in this total were several steam in various stages of preservation, class 2 2–6–0 No. 6441 being resplendent in maroon livery and fully restored, together with class 4 2–6–4 tank No. 42073 under restoration with a sign board on its buffer beam stating 'THE LAKESIDE RAILWAY SOCIETY'. To see '9F' class 2–10–0s waiting disposal at this depot was a sad sight: they had had under ten working years of service on BR and were certainly not worn out!

The ninth and final visit was to Springs Branch (Wigan) (8F), a coach journey of about 40 miles from Carnforth. As it was my final BR locomotive depot visit, I have included the complete list of notings:

Steam: 44678, 45198, 45226, 45281, 45331, 45368, 45431, 48061, 48637 and 48675.

Diesels: 12003, 12004, 12013, 12020, 12031, 12032 and D7556.

17 locomotives noted.

All the steam and diesels were redundant, waiting to be towed away, and were noted in the yard accompanied by numerous wagons and vans also destined for the breaker's yard. The doors on the main depot building at that time were closed, as it was being converted to a diesel depot.

For us trainspotters from southern England it had been an intensive day: thirteen hours travelling by coach, nine depots visited and many miles on shanks's pony. Despite the scene of gloom that descended whenever we visited an engine shed, the coach party seemed in a remarkably jolly mood on the return journey to Manchester. A selection of songs, some quite vulgar, echoed out over the coach. We made silly faces at people as we passed and my last 'Play Up Pompey' gummed labels were stuck firmly to the coach windows! We probably did all this to counteract our previous sadness when visiting locomotive depots.

Unsurprisingly, when we returned to Manchester city centre at 7.30 p.m. the twenty-two of us were not only footsore and weary but also longing for a decent meal and a drink. The first thing we did was to split up into groups of four or five and find some cafés. My group found one easily and I enjoyed a welcome mixed grill. To pass the time before returning to Piccadilly station for the 12.10 a.m. overnight train to Euston, we played on some pinball machines in an amusement arcade for about an hour. Next we found a pub and sampled half pints of the local brew, and followed this with a visit to Manchester (Exchange) station. We noted two steam, class 5 4–6–0 No. 44910 and Standard class 5 4–6–0 No. 73133, both quietly simmering under the station roof. It was nearly eleven when we came across what I termed a 'trainspotter's menu' – a fish and chip shop. Needless to say, we all indulged in bags of grease and I still had some Tizer to wash it down with! Feeling more refreshed, we returned to Piccadilly station to rejoin the rest of the party, and boarded the train well before its departure time. In the warm carriage sleep soon overcame me and I remember little of the return journey.

The next morning I caught the 7.24 electric-unit train from Waterloo to Fratton, an uneventful journey providing me with some time to sit quietly, tuck into my last packet of crisps, remove my Tuf shoes from my aching feet – and reminisce over the previous day's visits. Not without a tear in my eye, I realised I had witnessed the passing of BR steam.

When I returned home that day with the sights and sounds of the weekend still fresh, I cast my mind back over the previous thirteen years in which I and my fellow companions had travelled all over the British Railways system pursuing our hobby, 'bunking' sheds, eluding the foreman and making our own enjoyment. I thought about my adventures with Eddie Rooke, firstly as a pillion passenger on his scooter and later as a passenger in the various cars he had owned from his eighteenth birthday. It dawned on me that these memories ought to be committed to publication and I made my mind up to go ahead with compiling a book about my hobby.

I bought a second-hand Olivetti typewriter and two reams of foolscap, and began typing what would be 860 pages of memories! I have tried to engage my family in the pleasures of trainspotting through various trips and holidays but today, neither my wife Ann nor my grown-up sons have the slightest interest in railways past or present. Sadly, I have had to look to my friends from the past if I have wanted to share railway-related conversation and travel.

However, by December 1998 I had achieved another ambition, which was to present my own slide show, and give talks to railway societies and clubs based on my two previous books. 'Diaries of a Trainspotter – 1955 to 1968' has proved to be a nostalgic evening's entertainment not only for committed railway enthusiasts but also for the general public who take a mild interest in steam trains. I provide the audience with countless views of engine sheds, stations, a trainspotter's social life and my camping escapades and I also display such items as my Brownie box camera, the Pompey gong, the gummed labels, my plastic mac, my original haversack and my Tuf shoes.

Whatever happened to . . .

Eddie Rooke On leaving Southern Grammar School, Portsmouth, he joined the National Provincial Bank. He is now retired, a keen gardener, and still interested in steam railways; we often visit railway installations together.

David Copus Another Southern Grammar old boy. He was the inspiration behind many of our railway trips, and drew up meticulous plans to visit railway installations, with both official and unofficial permits! David influenced the purchase of the Pompey gong and was the instigator of the Pompey gummed labels. He worked all his sadly short life for the Portsmouth Water Company at Bedhampton. He died in 1993, weeks before the publication of the first volume of *Diary of a Trainspotter*, and is much missed.

Trevor 'Haggis' Robson The oldest of our group and yet another Southern Grammar old boy. Trevor was a civil servant in Portsmouth Royal Naval Dockyard, later moving on to Bath. He remained out of touch for many years until contact was re-established following the publication of the *Diary of a Trainspotter* books. Located in Radstock, Somerset in the mid-1990s. He died in 2006.

Tony 'Inky' Ingram Youngest of my Southern Grammar friends. It is hard to believe he was a mere fifteen years old when he accompanied Eddie and me on our Western Region Rail Rover in 1961. He worked in Portsmouth Dockyard all his life and is now retired and living in Southsea. We occasionally meet in Southsea.

Charlie Best Another of the Southern Grammar crowd. He fell out of touch in the early 1960s, and many rumours (not suitable for this book) circulate about him! There have been occasional sightings of him locally.

T.F. 'Gaffer' Bleach The oldest of the Southern Grammar crowd. He was a student apprentice at the Brush Engineering Works in Loughborough in 1958 and later entered Birmingham College of Technology. What 'T.F.' stood for was never revealed and we always referred to him as 'Gaffer' – although it was thought his first name might be Terence. His whereabouts are unknown.

Frank Allen Attended Southsea Modern School. His interest in railways led him to employment on track work with British Railways in the early 1960s. He moved to the Birmingham area during his late teens, and lost contact. We were joyously reunited via the *Diary* books. After a career with BUPA, he moved into the guest-house business in the Cotswolds, but is now semi-retired and living in Stratford-on-Avon – on the site of the former engine shed.

Terry Hunt Also attended Southsea Modern School. The 'glamour boy' of our trainspotting group who always attracted the fairer sex! He worked in Portsmouth Dockyard in the naval stores for many years. Terry was an extremely keen footballer in his younger days, played in higher levels of the game, and in later years took on the role of coaching. Now the manager of the BR Social Club, Fratton, we still meet every month. He lives in Southsea.

Roger 'Domer' Wade Yet another of the Southsea Modern crowd. His lack of hair was conspicuous even as a teenager, hence the nickname! He was interested both in railways and in football, and he had a trial for Chelsea FC. He was a prolific goal-scoring centre-forward. He was employed for many years as a porter and ticket collector at Fratton and other local stations. Now retired, he lives in Southsea.

Bill Jenkins One of our original group of trainspotters. He joined the Army in the late 1950s for something to do, incorporating trainspotting trips when home 'on leave' from Harrogate. He was employed as a postman for many years in the Gosport area and is now semi-retired. Bill maintains a keen interest in modern-day traction and railway photography, and contributes regularly to *Railway Magazine*.

Jim 'Jimpy' Lawrence Having lost contact between 1967 and 1993; Jim is another of our group who was delighted to be in touch once again through the publication of the *Diary* books. He is now employed as a manager in a Southsea casino and lives in Portsmouth. We meet occasionally, he attended my railway slide show at Fratton in May 2008

Dave Bodenham. Dave lived only a few yards from Sooty Footbridge in Fratton. He decided to join the Army in 1959 and, like Bill Jenkins, joined us on our travels when on leave. His Army days ended in 1970 and he is now a professional photographer, living in Ston Easton, near Bath.

Doug Willis One of David Copus's many younger friends, along with Roy Davidson, Dave Woolley, Mike Chapman, Mike Dooley and Roy Wiltshire, among others. Doug worked as a fireman on British Railways, based at both Fratton and Eastleigh in the 1960s, and then joined the Army and trained as a chef for six years. Once again, we were reunited via the *Diary* books. We keep in contact, and often embark on railway trips together, since he maintains an interest in observing modern railways. He was employed for many years as a chef in a well-known Southsea music venue. Now employed as a carriage cleaner for South West Trains, based at Fratton.

Mike Yerbury Mike attended Eastney Modern School and joined us on many Sunday excursions. We lost contact in 1967 but were reunited in the early 1990s at a meeting of the Portsmouth Regional Group of the Mid-Hants Railway Preservation Society and are still in touch today. Mike lives in the Eastney district of Portsmouth.

Roger Emptage Roger was not a trainspotter but accompanied us nevertheless on almost every Pompey football excursion, a true PFC fan, and he still travels to every home game. Being in our company obviously gave him a mild interest in trains! Roger now resides in Earley, near Reading, and still keeps in touch. He has attended my railway slide shows whenever in the Reading area.